BBQ Days, BBQ Nights

Barbecue recipes for year-round feasting

Helen Graves

Hardie Grant

BOOKS

Nig

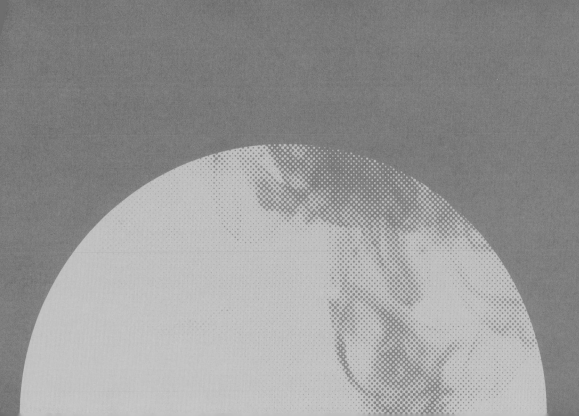

Introduction

The barbecue has been planned for weeks. There's a shopping list, a menu and a freezer full of ice. Friends have confirmed their attendance, their plus ones and their contributions. The event shimmers on the horizon like heat on a desert highway; potent and compelling.

The barbecue is spontaneous; an instinctive response to sunny weather and the reflexive desire to gather people. Let's have a good time. Let's all go back to mine? The idea fizzes with potential.

A barbecue is a chameleon, wearing different outfits. A shapeshifting scenario, it expands and contracts, straddling days, evenings, mealtimes and appetites. It resets rhythms and rekindles connections. There's a little bit of magic in every one, in the smells, sounds and sights; the long, lazy barbecue days and the heady barbecue nights.

For me, barbecue means cooking outdoors, often using seasonal ingredients and always embracing an informal way of eating. Do I enjoy eating at fancy restaurants? Absolutely yes. But when I'm having people over I want them to feel 100% at home un-self-consciously diving into that platter of nachos, splashing sauce on their clothes, and licking their fingers without embarrassment. I want them to know that they can pour drinks without having to ask and I want that food *demolished*.

BBQ Days, *BBQ Nights* is a celebration of socialising, connecting, and making other people happy through food. I want you to feel confident to invite people over and give you some fun ideas for food and drinks, whether you've got one hour or one week to prepare.

I noticed that the recipes readers loved most from my first book *Live Fire* were some of the simplest. The cookbook market is awash with titles aimed at saving time and effort and that is great, but I saw a slightly different way of approaching things. I heard from readers that they wanted *options*. Sometimes we want super simple last-minute ideas, other times we want to pull out all the stops (up to a point). The recipes in this book, then, are designed to be generous and accessible, boldly flavoured and satisfying.

They come in the form of sharing platters, easy cocktails, simple sides and big bowls or traybake desserts. If it's raining, there are options for cooking indoors. Sure, this is a book with barbecue recipes, but it's also a cookbook with adaptable methods. There's no way you're cancelling if it starts to rain. Bring it inside my friend! There are substitutions for my veggie pals and there are – I hope – clear and simple instructions across the board.

I've written all the recipes to serve 4 (and the occasional 4–6) with the option to double up for more people. And, if you want to scale down and a recipe can't be halved to serve 2, then you're going to have some lovely leftovers and that's never, ever, a bad thing. Basically, I just want you to cook from this book.

I strongly believe that good barbecued food – with a few notable exceptions – should be fun and not formal. We have Michelin-starred restaurants for the other end of the spectrum. Home entertaining, for me, is about sticky fingers, smoky hair and plenty of scrunched-up napkins. It's as much a way of cooking as it is a state of mind. Let me show you how I do it.

How it works

I've spent a lot of time feeding people, and I've found that there are only three time periods that really mean anything when it comes to entertaining.

- **Last minute** by which I mean anything up to an hour before people arrive, or maybe you are already with your guests and have made a spur of the moment decision to have a barbecue. Why not? Don't panic!
- **Tomorrow** meaning you have an overnight period where ingredients can marinate, you have a bit more time to prep and you have more options on the shopping side of things.
- **Up to a week in advance** for when you have the luxury of time to do pretty much anything you like. The freedom!

Indoor cooking instructions

I've provided indoor cooking instructions wherever possible because not everyone wants to barbecue unless the sun is shining – I get it. I'd rather you had instructions for both indoors and outdoors so that you can enjoy the recipes, whatever the weather. Perhaps you want to just light the barbecue for the main event, and you'd rather not char that ingredient for a dip or a dessert outdoors. Again, I get it. I've got you.

Suggested menus

I've arranged the book by season, because, you know, that's how time works, but you can obviously mix and match the recipes. Don't feel restricted. I've made suggestions for substitutions wherever possible, and I'd love to hear your ideas too if you've cooked from the book and come up with a fun twist I haven't considered. Get in touch via Instagram where I'm @FoodStories. This book was born from connecting with others, and I'd love to connect with you too. I like to keep things simple when I'm barbecuing, and the same goes when I'm entertaining. I tested every recipe in this book on a kettle barbecue with a lid, and it's the barbecue I use most often.

How to set up your barbecue

Lighting your barbecue

Place a natural wool fire lighter on the base of your barbecue (remove the grill first), then fill up your chimney starter with lump wood charcoal (see Stockists on page 16). Light the fire lighter, then place your full chimney on top of it and wait for 5–10 minutes before tipping the coals into the base of the kettle.

Barbecue setup

There's really only one setup your need to know about, and that's a two-zone setup for 'indirect cooking'. This just means that the coals are banked to one side of the barbecue creating a hot zone and a cooler zone. The hot zone can be used for searing and quick cooking, while the cooler zone is used for cooking larger bits of meat, for example, cooking things through more slowly and gently, and serves as a safe place to put things when they're cooking too fast and/or flames are flaring up due to dripping fat.

The only time I really deviate from this setup is when I'm cooking wings, when I arrange the coals in the centre of the barbecue with an empty ring around the outside. It's the same principle as above, but there's just extra room to cook more wings evenly at the same time.

On the occasions that I specify heat level in a recipe, 'medium-hot' simply means adding more coals, while 'medium-low' means adding – you've guessed it – fewer.

Barbecue equipment

These are the pieces of equipment I use most often and will genuinely make your life easier.

- **Chimney starter** A tall cylindrical mug-shaped vessel for lighting charcoal quickly and safely.
- **Long tongs** It's just easier to turn stuff when your hand isn't right over the fire (duh), so I recommend buying a pair with long handles.
- **Heatproof gloves** Really handy (lol) for when you're using things like a cast-iron skillet to make the Focaccia on page 124.
- **Cast-iron frying pan (skillet)** Affordable, durable and heatproof, cast-iron skillets are perfect for cooking bread, cakes and small things that might fall through the grates.
- **Fish cage** Very handy, particularly if you're nervous about turning fish on the grill.
- **Probe thermometer** Sometimes you just need to know what's going on inside, for example, a large piece of meat like the pork shoulder on page 84. This is where a decent quality probe thermometer like a Thermapen will be your best friend.
- **Long metal skewers** Reusable, durable and so much better than wooden sticks.

Kitchen equipment
- **Mini blender** A small 900 ml (30 fl oz) capacity blender is one of my most-used kitchen appliances, full stop. You will find it crops up throughout this book and I promise you it's one of the best pieces of kit you can own. It makes such short work of dips, marinades and sauces and is easy to store and clean.
- **Cocktail shaker and strainer** I use a very basic cocktail shaker, Hawthorne strainer and jigger. You won't need fancy equipment to make the drinks in this book.

Ingredients and stockists

● **Chilli** Yes, I love chilli. However, I hope you can see that I am usually attempting to extract the perfume of the chilli rather than much of the heat, for example in the Jalapeño Syrup on pages 103 and 112. From the sappy, aromatic green varieties to the fruity bulbous bonnets, I love them all. I would be surprised if you'd need to reduce the quantities in any of these recipes, but as always, you choose your own path!

● **Fresh herbs** All quantities for fresh herbs come in handfuls because there is no point using a small amount of any herb unless it's very strong (e.g., sage, rosemary) in my opinion. Please do be generous.

● **Salt** I use Maldon flaky sea salt, which I buy in catering-sized tubs. This is the salt I've used for every recipe in this book.

● **MSG** There are a couple of recipes that call for MSG, and I know there is still stigma around this ingredient. There shouldn't be. Please read Cheryl Chow's piece on MSG's history at *pitmagazine.uk/ features/my-grandmother-does-not-cook-for-the-white-gaze*

Some of my favourite store-bought condiments and crisps

● **The Eaten Alive range**, especially the scotch bonnet hot sauce and smoked sriracha. I have many hot sauces in my cupboard, but these are the constants.

● **Vadasz Jalapeño relish** is amazing on burgers, hummus and literally anything else. They also make great pickles.

● **Lao Gan Ma Chilli Crisp Oil** is an iconic chilli oil that's available in Asian supermarkets and larger supermarket branches in the UK.

● **Belazu rose harissa** is something I often stir through dips, add to marinades and spread into sandwiches. There is some really bad harissa out there, but this is a belter.

● **Odysea pomegranate molasses** is more an ingredient than a condiment, but really superb and a fantastic brand in general.

● **Luchito tortilla chips** are easily the best of the widely available range – they're really large, so great for scooping, and have a proper, traditional corn flavour. Beautiful.

● **Tajín** is a Mexican seasoning made with chilli, lime and salt. It's perfect for rimming cocktail glasses, seasoning tacos, eating with charred fruit, grilled seafood such as squid, and much more.

A note on crisps

When choosing crisps, do consider the consistency of the dip. A thicker dip, like, for example, the OTT Cod's Roe Platter on page 162 or the Elite Cream Cheese, Garlic and Chive Dip on page 166, will call for something sturdy, such as a crinkle cut. A runnier dip is more forgiving and will be perfectly happy alongside a Pringle. If there are chunky bits involved, it's often wise to go with a tortilla chip, which are unsurpassed in their ability to transport both liquid dip and solids into your mouth; a genuine all-star.

I usually go for a 'safe' option like one of the above, then get a wild card, which may or may not be the hit of the day/evening.

Charcoal

Do not buy cheap charcoal if you can help it. The cheap stuff is nasty, often made with trees from illegally felled rainforest, and is full of chemicals that then need to burn off before cooking. Good-quality charcoal lights faster, burns cleanly, and you can top it up during cooking without nasty flavours getting into your food.

There are loads of people making great quality charcoal from 100% British wood nowadays, so have a look around. Here are a couple of my favourites.

- **The Green Olive Firewood Co** greenolivefirewood.co.uk
- **Whittle & Flame** whittleandflame.co.uk

Spr

ring

Hot peas squeak as pods blister, insides rendered sweet. Spud-skins wrinkle and twinkle with salt, waxy flesh smoked. Crushed, they're drenched in nutty butter, for irresistible appeal. Asparagus, now shriveled-tender, is at its best. How much wobbly-fresh mayo can each jiggling spear hold? Skinny spring chops spit fat onto embers, each puff of smoke a signal drawing friends ever closer. We're in the mood for finger food. Let the good times roll.

Today

Spring

Drinks
Salty Dogs with Basil and Tarragon

Nibbles
Chilli Crisp Popcorn

Dip
Creamy Corn and Kimchi Dip

Platter
Sticky Chicken Wings (or Tenderstem) with
Grapefruit, Tamarind and Lime Leaf Dressing

Side
Curried Brown Butter Potato Salad with
Quick Pickled Corn

Dessert
Grilled Crumpets with Charred Pineapple
and Rum and Maple Caramel

Tomorrow

Next week

Drinks
Burnt Bonnet Lageritas

Nibbles
Very Moreish Charred Peas

Dip
Spring Green Queso

Platter
Smoky Pork Belly Tacos with Charred Pineapple
and Drunken Salsa

Side
Burnt Shallots, Butter Beans and Salsa Macha

Dessert
Chocolate Mousse, Sour Cream and
Tamarind Caramel

Drinks
Watermelon, Mint and Lemongrass Punch

Nibbles
Radishes with Seaweed Salt and
Szechuan Pepper Butter

Dip
Avocado, Cucumber and Candied Green
Chilli Dip

Platter
Cambodian-style Beef or Pumpkin Skewers
with Frazzled Basil

Side
Spring Green Soba with Asparagus and
Crispy Garlic

Dessert
Banana, Coffee and Tahini Cream Pudding

Drinks

Salty Dogs
with Basil and Tarragon

Makes: 4, easily doubled (with enough simple syrup for round 2)
Prep: The sugar syrup can be made up to a month in advance and refrigerated
Mixing time: 5 minutes
Equipment: Tall glass or vessel for mixing
Glass: Tall, like a Collins glass

---

handful of basil leaves
handful of tarragon leaves
75 ml (2½ fl oz/5 tablespoons) simple syrup (see below)
200 ml (7 fl oz/scant 1 cup) gin
400 ml (14 fl oz/generous 1½ cups) pink grapefruit juice
15 ml (½ fl oz/3 teaspoons) lime juice, plus extra to taste

Simple syrup
200 g (7 oz/generous 1 cup) caster (superfine) sugar
100 ml (3½ fl oz/scant ½ cup) water

To serve
lime wedges, for rimming the glasses
flaky sea salt
plenty of ice cubes
tarragon leaves
grapefruit peel

I'm a big fan of a long drink with hard liquor in it. Spicy enough to get the party started but an ample amount in the glass to keep people occupied while you sort nibbles. A Salty Dog is usually made with just grapefruit and gin (the same ingredients as a Greyhound but with the addition of a salted rim). I love adding tarragon and basil to mine; the drink becomes something more fragrant and intriguing while remaining, at its core, a mega-refresher. You won't be surprised to learn that it's also perfect for hot summer weather.

● Make the simple syrup by combining the sugar and water in a saucepan and heating gently until the sugar has dissolved. Allow to cool before using (do this over a bowl of ice if you're in a hurry).
● Combine the simple syrup and herbs in a tall glass or jug and use a cocktail muddler or something long like a rolling pin to push down and twist on the herbs in order to extract the flavour. Really get in there, twisting and mashing.
● Rim your serving glasses with salt by running a wedge of lime around the top edge. Sprinkle some salt onto a small plate and dip the rims into it. Fill each glass with a few ice cubes. Add the gin and grapefruit juice to the jug and mix well. Add the lime juice, mix, taste and add more if you like. Pour the drink over the ice into the salt-rimmed glasses and add the tarragon leaves and grapefruit peel.

Drinks

Burnt Bonnet Lageritas

Makes: 4 (to double this, make the same quantity of syrup but double the remaining ingredients. Store the syrup as below)
Prep: Minimum 1 hour syrup infusion time. The syrup can be made up to a month in advance and refrigerated. Mix the drink once people arrive.
Mixing time: 10 minutes
Glass: Tall, like a Collins glass

100 ml (3½ fl oz/scant ½ cup) tequila blanco
50 ml (1¾ fl oz/3½ tablespoons) Cointreau
50 ml (1¾ fl oz/3½ tablespoons) lime juice
50 ml (1¾ fl oz/3½ tablespoons) sugar syrup (see below), or to taste
1 litre (34 fl oz) lager or light IPA

Burnt bonnet sugar syrup
1 scotch bonnet chilli
200 g (7 oz/generous 1 cup) caster (superfine) sugar
100 ml (3½ fl oz/scant ½ cup) water

To serve
lime wedge
flaky sea salt
Tajín seasoning (or a little chilli powder)
plenty of ice cubes

This is another drink for people who don't have the time or inclination to make complicated cocktails (Me! Almost always!). It doesn't even require a shaker. The combination of light bubbly lager, the viper bite of tequila and fruity sting of bonnet is exciting and refreshing all at once.

One of my missions when using scotch bonnet chilli is to extract its sweet perfume. Yes, it's a hot chilli and it will add spice, but using it in a syrup means there's plenty of sweetness, which tempers the fire.

● Fry the scotch bonnet chilli in a dry frying pan (skillet) over a high heat for a few minutes, turning it regularly, until charred all over (of course, you could do this on the barbecue, but personally I wouldn't light it *just* to briefly char one chilli…).
● Add the scotch bonnet to a saucepan with the sugar and water. Stir over a low heat until the sugar has dissolved, then set aside to infuse for at least 1 hour (or overnight).
● Strain out the scotch bonnet and transfer the syrup to a sealed container.
● Run a lime wedge around the rims of your glasses. Combine some sea salt with Tajín seasoning then spread the mixture out on a plate before dipping the glasses rim side down until coated. Fill the glasses with ice cubes.
● In a jug, combine the tequila, Cointreau, lime juice and sugar syrup and mix well.
● Divide between glasses and top up with the lager or IPA.

Drinks

Watermelon, Mint and Lemongrass Punch

Makes: 4, easily doubled
Prep: 10 minutes, plus cooling time
Mixing time: 5 minutes
Equipment: Blender
Glass: Tall, like a Collins glass

half a 2–2.5 kg (4 lb 8 oz–5 lb
8 oz) watermelon, halved then
quartered (plus extra wedges
to garnish, if you like)
handful of mint leaves
100 ml (3½ fl oz/scant ½ cup)
tequila blanco
plenty of ice cubes

For the syrup
125 g (4½ oz/generous ½ cup)
caster (superfine) sugar
125 ml (4¼ fl oz/generous ½ cup)
water
125 ml (4¼ fl oz/generous ½ cup)
fresh lemon juice (buy at least
10 lemons for this)
grated zest of 1½ of the lemons
1 lemongrass stalk, outer layer
removed and then stalk bashed
to release the oils

Is serving punch at a party a statement of intent? Possibly.
This is going to be a lively one... That said, this isn't a back-of-the-
booze-cabinet pot pourri. Watermelon makes one of the best
juices, but it does need to be freshly made, and if you're going
to blend a watermelon, then you should put it to very good use.
This is so easy, and, obviously, also ideal for sweaty summer days.

● Combine the sugar and water for the syrup in a saucepan and
heat gently until the sugar has dissolved. Add the lemon juice,
zest and lemongrass to the syrup and set aside to cool.
● Blend the watermelon flesh and mint, then pass through
a sieve into a bowl or jug, pressing down on the solids to extract
all the juice.
● Combine the watermelon mixture with the tequila.
● Fill your glasses with ice cubes, then add 25 ml (¾ fl oz/
generous 1½ tablespoons) syrup to each glass. Top up with the
watermelon and tequila mixture and garnish with a watermelon
wedge, if you like.

Nibbles

Chilli Crisp Popcorn

Serves: 4, easily doubled
(if scaling up, bear in mind
that you might need to pop
it in two batches)
Prep: Pop the corn shortly before
or after guests arrive to ensure it's
still slightly warm. It takes so little
time to put together.
Cook and assembly time:
10 minutes

1 tablespoon vegetable oil
1 tablespoon chilli crisp oil
(I like to use Lao Gan Ma)
50 g (1¾ oz) popcorn kernels
flaky sea salt

This is super weird, but I didn't realise until recently that popping corn is widely available in supermarkets. I know! Of course, I embarked on a popcorn journey, making buttery sauces and, occasionally, terrible claggy mistakes involving too much sugar. The thing about popcorn is that it's supposed to be moreish, not overwhelming. I like mine with some spice (no surprises there) so I pop it in Lao Gan Ma chilli crisp oil, which you can buy in East Asian grocery shops or in larger supermarkets. It's jarred umami, and also a winner on grilled vegetables such as asparagus and broccoli, or shellfish like prawns (shrimp) and scallops. Warning: this popcorn is addictive.

● Add the two oils to your largest heavy-based saucepan (if you're worried about size, do it in 2 batches) over a medium heat, along with a few popcorn kernels. When they pop, add the rest of the kernels and put the lid on, leaving a small gap on one side (this will keep the popcorn dry and crisp).
● Shake the pan every so often, until the kernels stop popping.
● Transfer to a large bowl, leaving behind any burnt bits of chilli crisp in the pan. Season immediately and generously with salt. Serve warm.

Nibbles

Radishes
with Seaweed Salt and Szechuan Pepper Butter

Serves: 4, easily doubled
Prep: The butter and seaweed salt can both be made a day or two in advance. Store the butter in the fridge, well wrapped, and the salt in an airtight container. Radishes can be washed and dried ahead of time and chilled
Cook and assembly time:
5–10 minutes

20 radishes, washed and dried (keep them in the fridge)

Butter
1 teaspoon Szechuan peppercorns
75 g (2½ oz/5 tablespoons) butter, softened

Seaweed salt
1½ tablespoons dulse seaweed flakes (or 1 sheet of nori seaweed, blitzed in a spice grinder or blender)
1½ tablespoons flaky sea salt

Just when you think you've eaten your favourite radish and butter combo... hello! This is my all-time favourite way to serve what seems like a modern classic, because the tingly peppercorns and toasted dulse are a perfect match. The dulse becomes a little smoky given some heat, and the two seasonings smothered onto a crisp, cold radish... well. Try it and see what I mean. You could serve some bread with these to bulk it out, if you like.

● Heat a frying pan (skillet) over a medium heat and toast the Szechuan peppercorns for a minute or two until fragrant, tossing the pan to make sure they don't burn. They should smell lovely and citrusy.
● Lightly crush the peppercorns in a pestle and mortar (or just use the back of a spoon) and mix well with the softened butter. Chill until needed.
● Toast the dulse seaweed flakes briefly in a dry pan, just until fragrant. Mix with the salt.
● To serve, arrange the washed and dried radishes on a platter alongside pots of Szechuan pepper butter and seaweed salt for dipping.

Nibbles

Very Moreish Charred Peas

Serves: 4–6
Prep: Make the seasoning up
to a day ahead and store in an
airtight container
Cook and assembly time:
10 minutes
Equipment: Long metal skewers

500 g (1 lb 2 oz) sugar snap peas
small splash of neutral oil,
for cooking

Seasoning
1 tablespoon shelled unsalted
pistachios
1 tablespoon unsalted almonds
or peanuts
½ tablespoon sesame seeds
½ teaspoon ground coriander
½ teaspoon ground cumin
½ teaspoon onion flakes
½ teaspoon dried chilli flakes
½ teaspoon nigella seeds
½ teaspoon fennel seeds
pinch of MSG (optional)
a few generous pinches of flaky
flaky sea salt

I rather boldly opened my last book, *Live Fire*, with a plate of charred peas, then promptly wondered what I'd done. Thankfully (surprisingly) the recipe was incredibly popular, so I've brought them back for round two. Here, sugar snaps are briefly grilled then tossed with an addictive mixture of nuts and spices, which is part dukkah, part Everything Bagel Seasoning.

The ingredients are not set in stone – don't for a minute think 'oh no I don't have any nigella seeds, so I cannot make this' but I will say that the sesame, fennel and chilli work particularly well. Salt is, obviously, non-negotiable.

● Prepare a barbecue for charring the peas over direct heat.
● Make the seasoning by combining all the ingredients in a bowl or jar and mixing well.
● Toss the peas with a small splash of oil, thread onto long metal skewers then char over direct heat for a few minutes, or until lightly charred.
● Toss with the seasoning to serve.

To cook indoors: Preheat a griddle pan over a high heat for 5 minutes, then char the peas in the same way (minus the skewers).

Dips

Creamy Corn and Kimchi Dip

Serves: 4–6
Prep: Take the cream cheese out of the fridge 30 minutes before using, if possible. The dip is best made close to serving
Assembly time: 10 minutes

250 g (9 oz) kimchi
200 g (7 oz/generous ¾ cup) cream cheese
150 g (5½ oz/scant ⅔ cup) sour cream
1 teaspoon caster (superfine) sugar
1 teaspoon rice vinegar
1 × 200 g (7 oz) tin sweetcorn, drained
2 teaspoons soy sauce
2 spring onions (scallions), very finely chopped
pinch of flaky sea salt

This is a version of Hawaiian 'kimchee dip'; I like to add sweetcorn to mine, for a whiff of creamed corn. The most important part of this recipe is squeezing the kimchi as dry as possible, otherwise you end up with a watery dip and what you want is something thick and luscious. This is glorious with crisps, cucumber slices, pretzels, a spoon…

For a super quick fix along the same lines as this dip, blend equal amounts of crème fraîche with drained, blitzed kimchi.

● If you have a brand new or very clean cloth, place the kimchi into it and squeeze out as much of the juice as possible. If you don't have a cloth, use your hands. It's important to really squeeze it dry. Once dry, finely chop.
● Combine the cream cheese, sour cream, sugar and vinegar in a bowl and beat together (just with a spoon is fine) until lovely and smooth.
● Stir through the corn, soy sauce, kimchi and three-quarters of the spring onions (scallions). Taste for seasoning and adjust if necessary.
● Transfer to a serving bowl, and top with the remaining spring onions to serve.

Spring Green Queso

Serves: 6
Prep: The paste can be made
and the cheeses grated an hour
or two ahead
Cook and assembly time:
25 minutes
Equipment: Small blender,
heatproof serving dish such as
a cast-iron skillet

2 garlic cloves
6 spring onions (scallions),
green and white parts separated
1 fresh green chilli
large handful of coriander
(cilantro) leaves, plus a few extra
for garnish
80 g (2¾ oz) watercress (the usual
supermarket bag weight in the UK
– a bit more or less won't matter)
splash of neutral oil
1 large red onion, peeled and
thinly sliced
1 × 150 g (5½ oz) garlic and herb
Boursin garlic and herb cheese
150 g (5½ oz) mature Cheddar,
grated
150 g (5½ oz) Emmental, grated
lime wedges, to serve

Ideas for dipping
blanched or grilled asparagus
endive leaves
tortilla chips
radishes

I make this when I want something a bit green, but there's
still a nip in the air – it's a skillet of bubbling cheese, after all.
My best mate Holly says that I am incapable of writing a book
that doesn't contain at least two recipes using Boursin garlic and
herb cheese. She's right. In this book, there are three.

If wild garlic is in season, a handful of that would be lovely
in here. Add it to the paste with the watercress and omit the two
garlic cloves.

● Prepare a barbecue for two-zone cooking as described
on page 12, with medium-low heat.
● Put the garlic, white spring onions (scallions), green chilli,
coriander (cilantro) and watercress in a small blender and
whizz to a paste.
● Add a splash of oil to a serving skillet or pan set over the hot
coals and add the onion. Cook for 5–10 minutes until it's just
beginning to colour, then add the Boursin and allow it to melt
in, stirring.
● Spread the onion and Boursin mixture over the base of the
skillet, then add a big handful of the grated cheeses, plus a layer
of the green paste, then repeat with another two layers. Move the
skillet to the cooler side of the barbecue, close the lid and leave to
cook for 5–10 minutes or until everything is melted and bubbling.
● Finely chop the green parts of the spring onions then sprinkle
them on top with the a little extra coriander.
● Serve with the lime wedges and your choice of dippers.

To cook indoors: Cook indoors on the hob over a medium heat,
following the instructions above.

Avocado, Cucumber and Candied Green Chilli Dip

Serves: 4, easily doubled
Prep ahead: The crema can be made the day before and refrigerated, and the candied chillies can be made up to a week in advance and stored in the fridge
Cook and assembly time: 20 minutes
Equipment: Small blender

Cucumber
½ cucumber
1 teaspoon flaky sea salt
grated zest and juice of ½ lime

Candied green chillies
100 g (3½ oz/scant ½ cup) caster (superfine) sugar
½ teaspoon flaky sea salt
50 ml (1¾ fl oz/3½ tablespoons) white wine vinegar
100 g (3½ oz) fresh green chillies or jalapeños, de-stemmed and thinly sliced

Avocado crema
2 ripe avocados
juice of 1 lime
1 garlic clove
dash of hot sauce
4 tablespoons sour cream
Sea salt, to taste

To serve
300 g (10½ oz/1¼ cups) sour cream
tortilla chips

Big fan of layered dips over here *waves*. They look much fancier than regular dips because you can see all the different elements – think about eating a plate of food where everything is distinct as opposed to mixing it together into one big slop. They're also more fun to eat because you're getting different proportions of each element with every mouthful. No-one can say I don't know how to have a good time!

● Split the cucumber lengthways and use a teaspoon to scoop out the seeds. Cut the cucumber lengthways into thin strips and then finely dice it. It's worth taking time to get it nice and fine. Toss with the salt and transfer to a sieve to drain while you make the other elements.
● To make the candied green chillies, combine the sugar, salt and vinegar in a saucepan and heat until the sugar has dissolved, then simmer for 5 minutes. Add the chillies and bring back to the boil then reduce to a simmer and cook for another few minutes. Remove from the heat and allow to cool.
● Make the avocado crema by destoning and peeling the avocados, then putting them in a small blender with the lime juice, garlic, hot sauce and sour cream, blending until completely smooth. Season with salt.
● Rinse the cucumber and pat dry with kitchen paper, then toss with the lime juice and zest.
● Spread the sour cream over one or two serving plates and top with the crema, cucumber, then as many of the candied green chillies as you like (have a taste of everything together, then add some more if you love them – I like to add loads). Serve with tortilla chips.

Platters

Chicken Wings or Tenderstem
with a Grapefruit, Tamarind and Lime Leaf Dressing

Serves: 4, easily doubled
Prep time: The dressing and shallots can both be prepared a day in advance and refrigerated
Cook and assembly time: 40 minutes for chicken wings, 20 minutes for broccoli, plus infusing time
Equipment: Sieve, tongs

15 chicken wings, jointed to make 30 pieces, or 400 g (14 oz) Tenderstem broccoli
neutral oil, for cooking
1 fresh red chilli, very thinly sliced
handful of mint leaves, roughly chopped
handful of coriander (cilantro) leaves
flaky sea salt

Makrut lime leaves are key to the flavour of this aromatic dressing, and they do need to be fresh rather than dried. Buy them in South East Asian grocery shops in the freezer section, in larger supermarkets or online, then stash them in your own freezer where they'll keep for yonks.

This dish really pings around your palate – perfumed lime, sweet honey and sour tamarind, plus plenty of vibrant herbs. It's very much 'my kind of food' and should have people licking their fingers after they've swooped them across the plate. It also works just as well – and I really do mean just as well – with Tenderstem broccoli.

● Put the grapefruit juice, lime leaves and garlic in a small saucepan and bring to the boil, then set aside to infuse for 1 hour, if possible (although 15 minutes is better than nothing). Strain to remove the lime leaves and garlic.
● For the quick pickled shallots, combine the rice vinegar, sugar and salt with the tap-hot water and stir until the sugar and salt have dissolved. Add the shallot rings and set aside.
● Add the fish sauce, tamarind and honey to the grapefruit juice and return to a high heat until reduced by half. Decant a quarter of the dressing into a separate bowl.
● When you're ready to cook the wings, prepare a barbecue for two-zone cooking as described on page 12, with the coals positioned in the centre. If using broccoli, you can just bank the coals to one side.

**Tamarind, grapefruit
and lime leaf dressing**
200 ml (7 fl oz/scant 1 cup)
pink grapefruit juice (from about
2 pink grapefruits)
10 fresh lime leaves, torn
3 garlic cloves, peeled and
smashed with the side of a knife
1 tablespoon fish sauce
2 teaspoons tamarind paste
3 tablespoons honey

Quick pickled shallots
50 ml (1¾ fl oz/3½ tablespoons)
rice vinegar
2 teaspoons caster (superfine)
sugar
1 teaspoon sea salt
120 ml (4 fl oz/½ cup)
tap-hot water
2 small shallots, peeled and
sliced into thin rings

● If using chicken, rub the wings with a little oil and season with plenty of salt. Place on the barbecue in a ring around the coals – they should be nice and close to the coals so that they cook slowly but are not over direct heat. Cook the wings for 20–30 minutes, or until crisp all over and cooked through. You can move them closer to the coals as they burn down, then give them a crisp up directly over the coals at the end. When the wings are nearly ready, toss with the small bowl of reserved dressing and return to the barbecue briefly to caramelise.

● If using broccoli, toss with a little oil and season with salt. Grill over direct heat, turning them often, for 3 minutes, or until charred and tender. Toss with the small bowl of reserved dressing and briefly caramelise.

● Gently reheat the remaining dressing and pour it over the wings or broccoli, tossing well to combine. Top with the sliced red chilli, herbs and pickled shallots, then give everything a good toss again, just before serving.

To cook indoors: Preheat the oven to 200°C (400°F/gas 6) for the chicken, and roast the wings for 45 minutes, tossing with the small bowl of reserved dressing 5 minutes before the end of cooking time. For the broccoli, preheat a griddle pan over a high heat for at least 5 minutes then griddle for 8–10 minutes until charred. Toss with the small bowl of dressing then briefly caramelise. Dress the chicken or broccoli and garnish as above.

Platters

Cambodian-style Beef or Pumpkin Skewers
with Frazzled Basil

Serves: 4, easily doubled
Prep: Beef or pumpkin can
be marinated up to 2 days
in advance
Cook and assembly time:
45 minutes, plus marinating time
Equipment: Pestle and mortar,
small blender, tongs, metal
skewers

500 g (1 lb 2 oz) sirloin steak,
diced, or 1 large Jap/Kent
pumpkin or butternut squash,
peeled and cut into 2.5 cm
(1 inch) dice
flaky sea salt
lime wedges, to serve

Kroeung paste
1 × 3 cm (1¼ inch) square thin slice
from block of dried shrimp paste
(belachan)
2 lemongrass stalks, tough outer
layers removed and stalks sliced
1 shallot, peeled
20 g (¾ oz) galangal, peeled
15 g (½ oz) fresh turmeric, peeled
5 garlic cloves, peeled
4 fresh lime leaves, ribs removed
and leaves thinly sliced
3 tablespoons neutral oil
1 tablespoon fish sauce
pinch of flaky sea salt

Frazzled basil
groundnut oil
bunch of Thai basil, leaves picked
3 tablespoons vegetable or
groundnut oil

These skewers are absolutely packed with flavour and really
benefit from a long marinade, if you have the time. They're
marinated in aromatic, lemongrass-heavy kroeung, a Cambodian
seasoning paste, which differs from many pastes in that it's cooked
before use. Don't skip the crisp Thai basil garnish if you can help
it – the leaves cook in seconds, crackling and twisting into
glimmering glass teardrops.

● Make the kroeung paste by toasting the shrimp paste in a dry
frying pan (skillet) over a medium heat for about 10 minutes until
it is dark on all sides. It will emit a powerful aroma, and I like
to open a window while I'm toasting it. Once this is done, crush
it to a powder with a pestle and mortar.
● Place the lemongrass, shallot, galangal, turmeric, garlic and
lime leaves in a blender with the oil and blitz to a coarse paste.
● Heat a frying pan (skillet) over a medium heat and add the
paste from the blender. Cook for about 10 minutes, stirring,
until the ingredients are just beginning to brown. Add the shrimp
powder and cook for a further minute or so, then transfer
everything back to the blender with the fish sauce and some
salt and process again to a paste. Allow to cool.
● If using pumpkin or squash, place in a pan of cold water, bring
to the boil and cook for 1 minute, then drain. Allow to cool.
● Rub the paste all over the squash or beef and marinate for
about 1 hour, or overnight in the fridge (and up to 2 days).
● Once you're ready to cook the skewers, prepare a barbecue for
two-zone cooking as described on page 12, with medium heat.
Season the beef or pumpkin with salt and thread onto skewers.
● Grill the beef or pumpkin skewers for about 5 minutes on each
side, or until charred in places and cooked through.
● Heat the oil in a frying pan over a medium heat. Add the basil
leaves and fry for 30 seconds before draining on kitchen paper.
Scatter the frazzled leaves over the skewers, squeeze over some
lime juice and add a final sprinkle of sea salt before serving.

Smoky Pork Belly Tacos
with Charred Pineapple and Drunken Salsa

Serves: 4–6, easily halved
Prep time: Marinate the pork belly
a day in advance if you have time.
Make the drunken salsa up to
8 hours in advance and keep
it in the fridge
Cook and assembly time:
1½ hours, plus marinating time
(if you can). Allow extra time
before cooking the pork if you
want to make your own tortillas
Equipment: Spice grinder or pestle
and mortar

Pork
1 kg (2 lb 4 oz) pork belly strips

Al pastor rub
1 dried ancho chilli
1 dried guajillo chilli
2 tablespoons ground cumin
2 tablespoons ground coriander
2 tablespoons flaky sea salt
2 tablespoons soft brown sugar
1½ tablespoons onion powder
1½ tablespoons annatto powder
1½ tablespoons garlic powder
2 teaspoons dried oregano

Drunken salsa
4 dried ancho chillies
2 dried pasilla chillies
1 × 330 ml (11 fl oz) can of IPA
6 tomatoes
1 onion, chopped
2 garlic cloves, peeled
50 ml (1¾ fl oz/3½ tablespoons)
orange or pineapple juice
generous pinch of salt

The rub for these tacos is based on the classic dish al pastor, which is traditionally made with pork and cooked on a kebab spit called a tromp, a cooking method that was introduced to Mexico by Lebanese immigrants. I've developed a version using pork belly strips, which cook very quickly and have a perfect fat to meat ratio in every bite. The key is to cook them away from the coals so that they become tender but the fat doesn't drip, causing massive flare-ups.

A note about tortillas: homemade will be a hundred times better than shop bought, definitely in terms of flavour but mainly in terms of texture. However, not everyone wants to make tortillas at home – I get it – so if you do use the pre-made ones, just make sure to warm them until they're soft and pliable, otherwise they will be crumbly, hard and weird.

● Toast the chillies for both the rub and the salsa in a dry frying pan (skillet) over a medium-high heat for a couple of minutes until fragrant and a little crisp, then split the chillies and remove the seeds and stalks. Grind the chillies for the rub to a powder and set the chillies for the salsa to one side.
● Combine all the ingredients for the rub (including the ground chillies) and mix well. Rub this all over the belly strips and transfer to the fridge to marinate overnight, or for as long as you can.
● To make the drunken salsa, first combine the dried whole chillies with the IPA and set aside for 20 minutes. Cut a cross in the base of the tomatoes and place in a heatproof bowl. Cover with boiling water and leave for 5–10 minutes until the skins start to peel back. Drain and skin the tomatoes.
● In a pestle and mortar or small blender, crush or whizz the tomatoes, onion and garlic to a coarse mixture. Add the chillies and IPA and pulse or crush until just combined. Pour the salsa into a bowl and mix in the pineapple or orange juice and salt.
● Combine the ingredients for the guacamole by destoning, peeling and mashing the avocados and seasoning really well

Guacamole
4 ripe avocados
juice of 1–2 limes
handful of coriander (cilantro)
leaves, chopped
flaky sea salt

Charred pineapple
1 pineapple, trimmed, peeled,
cored and cut into long wedges

To serve
corn tacos (4–5 per person if small
and homemade, 3–4 if using the
larger shop-bought ones)
2 onions, very finely diced
lime wedges
hot sauce

with salt and lime juice – seasoning generously is the key to
a good guac. Add the coriander (cilantro) and mix to combine.
● Prepare a barbecue for two-zone cooking as described on
page 12. When it's ready, place the pork belly strips on the cooler
side, away from the coals. Cook for 30 minutes with the lid closed
and bottom and top vents three-quarters closed, turning the strips
occasionally to ensure they cook evenly.
● Once the pork is cooked, briefly char the pineapple wedges
over direct heat – a couple of minutes on each side should do it.
● Slice the pork belly strips really thinly widthways and pile all
the meat onto a platter. Serve with the accompaniments and let
everyone build their own tacos.

To cook indoors: Cook the pork strips under a medium-hot grill,
taking care not to burn them. It's better to have the pork on a
slightly lower shelf here than to have it spitting and burning
before it's tender. They'll take about 30 minutes, turning them
once. Cook the pineapple wedges in a hot griddle pan until
charred – a few minutes on each side.

If you want to make your own tortillas: you'll need a tortilla
press, which is an inexpensive piece of kit widely available online.
Mix 500 g (1 lb 2 oz) masa harina with about 600 ml (20 fl oz/
2½ cups) water and two large pinches of salt to make enough
tortillas to serve 8 people. Bring the dough together into a smooth
round mass without lumps then wrap in cling film (plastic wrap)
and leave for 10 minutes. To cook, heat a cast-iron pan or
non-stick frying pan (skillet) over a high heat. Roll the dough into
golf-ball-sized pieces. Place a piece of baking paper into your
taco press and put a ball on top. Top with another sheet of paper
and press. Cook each one in the hot pan until the edges start to
look dry, then flip. The taco may start to puff up slightly and will
have a speckled appearance when it is ready. Stash the tacos in
a folded clean tea towel to keep them soft and warm.

Sides

Curried Brown Butter Potato Salad
with Quick Pickled Corn

Serves: 6
Prep: The potato salad and pickled corn can be prepared a day in advance, but combine them and add the herbs and crispy garlic chips just before serving
Cook and assembly time: 30 minutes

1.5 kg (3 lb 5 oz) Jersey Royals or other new potatoes
large handful of coriander (cilantro) leaves, chopped
large handful of chives, very thinly sliced
flaky sea salt and freshly ground black (and white, if you have it) pepper

Quick pickled corn
100 ml (3½ fl oz/scant ½ cup) white wine vinegar
200 ml (7 fl oz/scant 1 cup) tap-hot water
3 tablespoons caster (superfine) sugar
1½ tablespoons flaky sea salt
1 × 200 g (7 oz) tin sweetcorn, drained

Crispy garlic chips
75 g (2½ oz/5 tablespoons) butter
75 ml (2½ fl oz/5 tablespoons) olive oil
1 head of garlic, cloves peeled and thinly sliced
1½ tablespoons curry powder

I made this on a whim one afternoon and it's been a staple ever since. Soaking crushed new potatoes in toasty brown butter brings out the nuttiness of the tender spuds, and it becomes something so much more impressive than a mayo-based potato salad (not that I won't hoover up a mayo-based potato salad, don't get me wrong). There's warmth from the curry powder, zingy pickled corn and – my favourite part – crispy garlic chips. No point doing things by halves.

● Make the quick pickled corn by combining the vinegar, tap-hot water, sugar and salt in a bowl. Stir well until the sugar and salt have dissolved, then add the corn and set aside.
● If the potatoes are small, keep them whole, but halve or quarter any larger ones so they're all roughly the same size.
● Cook them in plenty of well-salted boiling water until tender, then drain.
● While the potatoes are cooking, melt the butter in a frying pan (skillet) over a medium heat and allow it to turn brown and nutty – this will take 2–3 minutes. Add the olive oil and the sliced garlic and cook for a few minutes until it begins to turn nice and golden around the edges, then remove and drain on kitchen paper (don't allow it to fully turn brown before removing, as it will continue cooking a little once drained, and overcooking will make it bitter). Add the curry powder and swirl it in the pan for 30 seconds, then remove from the heat.
● Once the potatoes are ready, drain well and lightly crush them, then transfer to a serving bowl. Add some more salt and plenty of pepper (I like a mixture of black and white). Pour the curried butter over the potatoes and mix well.
● Drain the pickled corn, then stir it through the potato salad with the herbs. Top with the crispy garlic chips just before serving.

Spring Green Soba
with Asparagus and Crispy Garlic

Serves: 4
Prep: The whole dish can be made a few hours ahead or even the day before – just make sure to add the crispy garlic chips right before serving. If making the garlic ahead, store in an airtight container at room temperature.
Cook and assembly time:
35 minutes
Equipment: Small blender

2 bundles of green asparagus, trimmed
neutral oil, for grilling
400 g (14 oz) soba noodles
1 tablespoon toasted sesame seeds
flaky sea salt

Crispy garlic chips
vegetable or groundnut oil, for cooking
1 head of garlic, cloves peeled and thinly sliced

Green sauce
6 spring onions (scallions)
large bunch of coriander (cilantro) leaves and stalks
120 g (4¼ oz) tahini
2 tablespoons lime juice
1 tablespoon fish sauce
2 tablespoons rice vinegar
1 tablespoon sesame oil

There's something so elegant about soba noodles, and here they're coated in a green sauce that's rich with sesame paste and fresh with coriander. I love to add chopped grilled asparagus to this when it's in season, but you could also use sugar snaps, mange tout (snow peas) or Tenderstem broccoli for a similar effect. Yes, I have a thing for crispy garlic.

● To make the crispy garlic chips, heat a 1 cm (½ inch) depth of oil in a frying pan (skillet) over a medium heat. Once hot, add the garlic slices and fry until just golden (don't fry them any more than this as they will turn bitter). Drain on kitchen paper.
● If grilling the asparagus, prepare a barbecue for two-zone cooking as described on page 12. If using a griddle pan, make sure it's preheated. Toss the asparagus with a little oil and season with salt, then grill over direct heat for a few minutes, or until blistered and softened. Chop into 2.5 cm (1 inch) pieces.
● Put the spring onions (scallions) and coriander (cilantro) in a small blender and process to a coarse paste. Add the tahini, lime juice, fish sauce and vinegar and process again – the texture will be a bit thick at this stage. Drizzle in 100 ml (3½ fl oz/scant ½ cup) of very cold water, with the motor running, until the dressing is smooth. Stir through the sesame oil and season with salt.
● Fill a large saucepan with boiling water and season it. Use two saucepans if you don't have a big one. Drop the noodles into the boiling salted water and cook for 4–5 minutes, giving them a good stir once they start to soften. They should still be al dente.
● Drain the noodles and transfer them to a bowl of cold water. Swoosh the noodles around with your hands for 1 minute. Drain.
● Combine the rinsed noodles with the sauce and the asparagus. Top with the garlic chips and sesame seeds just before serving.

To cook indoors: Preheat a griddle pan over a high heat for 5 minutes. Reduce the heat to medium. Prepare the asparagus as above, then griddle for 5 minutes until charred and soft.

Burnt Shallots, Butter Beans and Salsa Macha

Serves: 4, easily doubled
Prep: Make the salsa macha up to a week before, stored in a tightly sealed container in the fridge. The butter beans can be prepared several hours in advance, but heat them through gently and serve closer to room temperature
Cook and assembly time: 30 minutes
Equipment: Small blender or pestle and mortar, tongs

2 banana shallots, halved lengthways but skin left on
neutral oil, for brushing
olive oil, for frying
2 garlic cloves, grated
1 × 400 g (14 oz) tin butter (lima) beans, drained
splash of water or chicken/ vegetable stock (broth)
1 tablespoon sour cream
1 teaspoon red wine vinegar
flaky sea salt and freshly ground black pepper
lime wedges, to serve

This is a substantial, sexy side full of dark, roasted flavours to complement the sweetness of the shallots. Salsa macha harnesses the same magic as a Chinese crispy chilli oil, which is: lots of tasty BITS. This umami-laden crunch hides in every nook and cranny, ready to bring huge flavour. Try it in tacos, on eggs, with other grilled vegetables or shellfish. Plus – DIP ALERT! – leave a bag of tortilla chips knocking about and any remaining salsa will disappear.

- To make the salsa macha, first split the chillies lengthways and remove the seeds and stalks.
- Heat the oil in saucepan over a medium heat, add the garlic and cook for about 5 minutes until golden brown. Remove the garlic and discard.
- Add the peanuts to the oil and fry for a couple of minutes until golden. Remove and set aside.
- Cook the chillies in the oil until slightly darker in colour, then remove and set aside. Whizz the peanuts and chillies in a small blender or crush them using a pestle and mortar. Mix in the oil they were fried in, along with the vinegar, oregano and salt. Set aside.
- Prepare a barbecue for two-zone cooking as described on page 12.
- Brush the cut sides of the shallots with oil and place over direct heat on the barbecue. Cook for 10 minutes, then flip them with tongs and cook for 5 minutes skin-side down.
- Allow to cool a little, then peel and separate the petals, discarding the outer layers of skin.

Salsa macha

2 dried ancho chillies
4 dried chilli de arbol
100 ml (3½ fl oz/scant ½ cup)
light olive oil
3 garlic cloves, peeled and halved
50 g (1¾ oz) unsalted peanuts
1 teaspoon red wine vinegar
½ teaspoon dried oregano
generous pinch of flaky sea salt

● Heat a glug of olive oil in a frying pan (skillet) over a medium heat, add the garlic and soften for a few minutes, then tip in the butter (lima) beans. Add the splash of water or stock and cook gently for a couple of minutes until the beans are warmed through.

● Remove from the heat and add the sour cream, mixing it through well. Season with salt and pepper and set aside.

● To serve, spread the butter beans over a platter and top with the onion petals. Drizzle some of the salsa macha over the petals and transfer the rest to a dish to serve on the side for people to help themselves.

● Squeeze over lime juice just before serving.

To cook indoors: Preheat a griddle pan over a high heat for at least 5 minutes, then cook the shallots as above.

Grilled Crumpets
with Charred Pineapple and Rum and Maple Caramel

Makes: 8
Prep: The caramel can be made 24 hours in advance if you have the time. Store in an airtight container at room temperature
Cook and assembly time: 30 minutes
Equipment: Electric whisk, tongs

Crumpets
150 g (5½ oz/10½ tablespoons) unsalted butter
125 g (4½ oz/generous ½ cup) caster (superfine) sugar
1½ teaspoons vanilla bean paste
1½ teaspoons ground ginger
8 crumpets

Pineapple and caramel
1 ripe pineapple, trimmed
60 g (2¼ oz/4 tablespoons) unsalted butter
100 g (3½ oz/½ cup) soft light brown sugar
50 g (1¾ oz) maple syrup
2 tablespoons dark rum
1 tablespoon double (heavy) cream
pinch of flaky sea salt

Lime cream
300 ml (10 fl oz/1¼ cups) double (heavy) cream or whipping cream
grated zest of 1 lime
pinch of ground ginger
1 tablespoon caster (superfine) sugar

To serve
vanilla ice cream

These crispy caramelised sugary-buttered crumpets remind me a little of a kouign-amann, which is a type of French pastry with massive amounts of glorious fat and sugar nestled within its folds.

The idea for caramelising crumpets to use in a dessert was inspired by Ixta Belfrage's book *Mezcla*, in which she serves hers like a mini Black Forest gateau.

- Prepare a barbecue for two-zone cooking as described on page 12, with medium heat.
- Slice the pineapple into quarters lengthways then peel and remove the core. Chop each section in half widthways, then slice into 3 long wedges per section.
- Combine the butter and brown sugar in a frying pan (skillet) and heat for 2 minutes over a medium heat until bubbling. Stir in the maple syrup and cook over a medium heat for about 5 minutes until thickened. Stir in the rum, cream and salt. Set aside.
- Whip the cream, lime zest, ginger and sugar in a bowl with an electric whisk until soft peaks form. Keep chilled.
- Melt the butter for the crumpets in a frying pan over a medium heat and stir in the sugar, vanilla and ginger.
- Briefly grill the crumpets over direct heat on both sides until lightly toasted only (as they will be cooked again). Dunk them in the butter and sugar mixture, then return to the grill on the cooler side. Cook briefly again, until caramelised on both sides.
- Grill the pineapple wedges for a few minutes over direct heat until charred on all sides. Add the pineapple to the caramel.
- Serve the crumpets topped with a scoop of ice cream, the pineapple, the caramel sauce and a dollop of the cream.

To cook indoors: Preheat the oven to 220°C (430°F/gas 9) and line a tray with baking paper. Place the butter and sugar mixture-coated crumpets onto the baking tray and bake for 15 minutes until golden brown. To cook the pineapple, char briefly in a preheated griddle pan.

Chocolate Mousse, Sour Cream and Tamarind Caramel

Serves: 8, easily halved (or save any leftover for the day after... just an idea)
Prep: The chocolate mousse should be made at least 4 hours but ideally 24 hours before serving. The caramel can be made at least a few days before
Cook and assembly time: 30 minutes, plus setting time
Equipment: Electric whisk

4 egg yolks
60 g (2¼ oz/generous ¼ cup) caster (superfine) sugar
600 g (1 lb 5 oz) really good-quality dark chocolate, chopped
100 g (3½ oz/7 tablespoons) unsalted butter, at room temperature
pinch of chilli powder
12 egg whites
½ teaspoon lemon juice
pinch of flaky sea salt
sour cream, to serve

Tamarind caramel
175 g (6 oz/12 tablespoons) unsalted butter
1 × 397 g (14 oz) tin condensed milk
3 tablespoons golden (light corn) syrup
75 g (2½ oz/⅓ cup) dark muscovado sugar
2 tablespoons tamarind paste

The better quality your chocolate, the better your mousse. That is the most valuable piece of advice I can give you for making this stone-cold classic. You want that depth of flavour to complement the tangy caramel, which is SO good, by the way, you'll be sloshing it over everything.

You can add a couple of tablespoons of booze to the mousse if you like: coconut rum would be fun. Add it to the melted chocolate and butter before cooling.

● Whisk the egg yolks and sugar together in a bowl until they look pale and the mixture forms a ribbon when the whisk is lifted.
● Melt the chocolate with the butter in a heatproof bowl set over a pan of gently simmering water (don't let the water touch the bottom of the bowl), then stir in the chilli powder. Set aside.
● Whisk the 12 egg whites together in a clean bowl with the lemon juice and salt until they are barely at the soft peak stage.
● Check the chocolate is still warm to the touch. If it isn't, gently reheat it until it's just warm, not hot. Pour the melted chocolate mixture into the bowl of egg yolks and sugar and very briefly whisk to combine.
● Gradually fold the whipped egg whites into the chocolate mixture in four additions, making sure not to over mix.
● Decant into a large bowl and leave to set in the fridge for at least 4 hours but ideally overnight.
● To make the caramel, combine the butter, condensed milk, golden syrup and sugar in a saucepan and heat gently until smooth. Bring the mixture to the boil, then let it bubble for about 5 minutes until thickened, whisking it regularly to prevent the bottom from burning. Remove from the heat and whisk in the tamarind.
● Remove the mousse from the fridge 20 minutes before serving.
● Serve the mousse in big scoops, topped with some tamarind caramel and a spoonful of sour cream. Any leftover caramel can be kept for up to 2–3 weeks in the fridge.

Desserts

Banana, Coffee and Tahini Cream Pudding

Serves: 8
Prep: Layer up the dessert the day before but don't dust with cocoa powder until ready to serve
Cook and assembly time: 15 minutes
Equipment: Electric whisk

---

about 100 g (3½ oz) sponge fingers (ladyfingers)
300 ml (10 fl oz/1¼ cups) strong coffee, cooled
3 large bananas, peeled and sliced
cocoa powder, for dusting

Tahini cream
400 ml (14 fl oz/generous 1½ cups) double (heavy) cream
250 g (9 oz/generous 1 cup) mascarpone
75 g (2½ oz/scant ⅔ cup) icing (powdered) sugar
1 teaspoon vanilla extract or vanilla bean paste
80 g (2¾ oz) tahini, mixed well

This is what I mean by a 'big bowl dessert' – a few crowd-pleasing elements layered up and ready for attacking with your largest spoon. I generally make this in a small baking dish now, but the bowl point still stands. The flavours are quite grown up, but the essence of the dessert is childlike, which pleases me. It hugely benefits from being made the day before, so that everything has time to settle together.

● To make the tahini cream, whisk together the cream, mascarpone, icing (powdered) sugar and vanilla in a bowl until you have very soft and floppy peaks. Whisk in the tahini until just combined.
● Dip each sponge finger into the coffee until it's soaked but not soggy. Make a layer of fingers on the bottom of your serving dish (you will do 2 layers). Add a layer of bananas and tahini cream, then repeat each with a second layer. Refrigerate overnight.
● When you're ready to serve, dust with cocoa powder.

Sum

mmer

It's here, pals: the golden era. Bare toes tickled by soft summer grass, we blink into the light. Tongs snap as food sizzles. Groups giggle. Do you remember that time we cooked shawarma in the snow? Lazy summer days trump hazy winter memories. Skins burst as tomatoes shrivel. Juice runs over yoghurt dunes. Puffy breads swept by sticky fingers. Vegetables ripen, soon to be charred. Stone fruits soften; hot flesh jammy against cold whipped cream.

Menus

Today

Summer

Drinks
Mezcal and Maggi Micheladas

Nibbles
Hildas

Dip
Whole Roasted Courgette, Feta, Mint and Honey Dip

Platter
Grilled Bavette (or Portobellos) with Sour Creamed Corn and Lime Pickle Butter

Side
Gem Salad with Secret Weapon Dressing

Dessert
Tequila-macerated Strawberries with Salted Whipped Cream

Tomorrow

Next week

Drinks
Boozy Mango Slushies

Nibbles
Spicy Prawn Ceviche Cups

Dip
Charred Tomato 7-layer Dip

Platter
Charred Onion-Chermoula Prawns with
'Nduja, Ricotta and Fennel Butter Cornbread

Side
Grilled and Chilled Peppers with Harissa,
Pineapple and Lime

Dessert
Lemon, Jalapeño and Lemongrass Granita

Drinks
Tepache and Burnt Lime Coolers

Nibbles
Curried Crabby Nachos

Dip
Herb Garden Dip

Platter
Sticky Spiced Mango Pork Shoulder with
Mango Pickle

Side
Tomato Salad with Sizzled Ginger Dressing

Dessert
No-churn Vietnamese Coffee Ice Cream

Drinks

Tepache and Burnt Lime Coolers

Makes: 4, with lots of tepache left
Prep: The tepache takes between
24 and 36 hours to ferment, and I
like to leave mine for a few days,
until it's fizzy. The speed of the
ferment will depend on your
pineapple and the temperature
of the room
Cook and assembly time:
10 minutes, plus fermentation time
Equipment: Large jar for
fermentation (about 3-litre/
100 fl oz/12 ½ cup), clean
tea towel or muslin, tongs,
rubber band
Glass: Tall, like a Collins glass

50 ml (1¾ fl oz/3½ tablespoons)
lime juice (from 3–4 limes)
100 ml (3½ fl oz/scant ½ cup)
mezcal
400 ml (14 fl oz/generous 1½ cups)
tepache
ice cubes
sparkling water
lime peel

Tepache
150 g (5½ oz/¾ cup) caster
(superfine) sugar
1 ripe pineapple
2 scotch bonnet chillies, pierced
but left whole (optional)

Long, light and fizzy, this drink cools you instantly. It's unchallenging, yet very moreish. Tepache is a Mexican drink made from fermented pineapple peelings and it's so easy – just pop the peelings in a jar with sugar and water and let the magic happen. I like to let mine get quite fizzy, which means leaving it for a few days, but just have a taste and stop fermenting it when you're happy.

● For the tepache, combine the caster (superfine) sugar with 1.5 litres (50 fl oz/6¼ cups) of cold water in a large jar and stir until all the sugar has dissolved.
● Cut the top off the pineapple and discard it, then wash the outside of the pineapple with water. Trim off the pineapple peel and roughly chop it, then add the pieces to the jar with the scotch bonnet chillies (if using).
● Chop up the fruit and reserve it for another use (e.g., the Hildas on page 80), but add the core to the jar. Weigh the peelings down with a small (sterilised) dish or a fermentation weight. You could also use a sandwich bag filled with water. Cover the top of the jar with some muslin or a clean tea towel, secured with a rubber band – the idea is to let the mixture breathe but keep flies out. Set aside at room temperature for 24–36 hours. After 24 hours there might be some white foam on top of the liquid – gently remove it, then re-cover.
● Once the tepache is fermented to your liking, strain it into a container and refrigerate – a light fizz is my preference.
● Char your limes (that you'll be juicing) cut-side down, either in a hot griddle pan or on a barbecue, if it's lit already. They'll only take a couple of minutes. Combine the mezcal, lime juice and tepache in a jug, then pour over ice into glasses. Top up with sparkling water and garnish with lime peel.

Drinks

Mezcal and Maggi Micheladas

Makes: 4, easily doubled
Prep: I find this easier to make per glass then to prep as a batch, and it takes so little time to put together it's not really worth prepping in advance
Mixing time: 5 minutes
Glass: Tall, like a Collins glass

lime wedges
flaky sea salt
chilli powder
plenty of ice cubes
100 ml (3½ fl oz/scant ½ cup) mezcal (a shot per glass)
a few shakes of hot sauce per glass
a few cracks of black pepper per glass
a few drops of Maggi liquid per glass
a few drops of Worcestershire sauce per glass
about 400 ml (14 fl oz/generous 1½ cups) tomato juice
2 × 330 ml (11 fl oz) bottles or cans of light, bubbly lager or light IPA
4 tablespoons lime juice

Long, lagery drinks are just perfect for barbecues – all the refreshment of a beer but with a little extra somethin'. There are many ways of seasoning Micheladas but my favourite is Maggi: it's a concentrated seasoning liquid that's good because it contains MSG and therefore puts its foot on the umami throttle. There are two ways to go with this, depending on how you want to get the party started: mezcal or... no mezcal. I love the flavour of it here as much as the effects.

● Run a lime wedge around the edge of each glass. Spread a plate with flaky salt and a little chilli powder and dip the rims of the glasses into it.
● Add ice cubes to each glass, followed by mezcal, hot sauce, black pepper, Maggi and Worcestershire sauce. Top each up with half tomato juice, half lager/IPA and a tablespoon of lime juice.

Drinks

Boozy Mango Slushies

Makes: 8 (it's easier to make a larger amount then you necessarily need here – it's unlikely to go to waste)
Prep: Freeze the slushy mix 3–4 hours in advance
Cook and assembly time: 5 minutes
Glass: Short, like an Old Fashioned

grated zest and juice of 3 limes
850 g (30 oz) canned mango pulp (this comes in large tins at the supermarket or Asian grocers)
salt, to taste
alcohol of your choice, to serve (I usually use tequila)

My life changed forever the day I discovered canned mango pulp. I love making sorbets and boozy slushies with it, and it's so easy. These can go in many different directions, so look at this recipe as a starting point. Try adding your favourite booze, for example (vodka or gin work best if you want to keep it simple), while rum or coconut rum will bring a more tropical vibe. I also love the spice of tequila. You could add flavourings such as stem ginger syrup, or try infusing a simple syrup like the one on page 24 with different herbs – mint works really well.

● Combine the lime juice, mango pulp and salt and mix well. Taste, and adjust if necessary.
● Transfer to a lined freezerproof container, seal and place into the freezer for 3–4 hours, until it has a slushie consistency. Give it a good stir and transfer to glasses. Add a shot of alcohol to each and mix, then top with a little lime zest.

Dips

Charred Tomato Seven-Layer Dip

Serves: 6
Prep: The creamy base layer, apricot salsa and sun-dried tomatoes with harissa can all be prepped several hours in advance and chilled.
Cook and assembly time: 30 minutes
Equipment: Tongs, small blender

500 g (1 lb 2 oz) cherry tomatoes on the vine
125 g (4¼ oz) feta, crumbled
1 tablespoon pomegranate molasses
sea salt and freshly ground black pepper

Pickled apricot salsa
generous 1½ teaspoons lemon juice
2 teaspoons maple syrup or honey
50 g (1¾ oz) dried apricots, diced
handful of mint leaves, chopped
handful of basil leaves, chopped
2 tablespoons extra virgin olive oil

Creamy base layer
juice of ½ lemon
2 garlic cloves, grated to a paste
150 g (5½ oz/¾ cup) cream cheese
150 g (5½ oz/¾ cup) natural yoghurt

Sundried tomato and harissa layer
100 g (3½ oz) sundried tomatoes
3 tablespoons good-quality harissa (I use Belazu)
squeeze of lemon juice

I've always loved the concept of a seven-layer dip but not the reality; it seemed to be style over substance, and, to be honest, not that much style. But who said the layers have to be true to the original? The most popular recipe in my previous book, *Live Fire*, was the Charred Tomatoes with Yoghurt, so I'm revisiting the vibe in a new, fun form. It's like the original got a major glow up with an extra creamy base, a pickled apricot salsa and an extra harissa layer. It's even messier, and triumphant with bold flavours.

- Prepare a barbecue for two-zone cooking as described on page 12.
- First, make the pickled apricot salsa. Combine the lemon juice, honey or maple syrup and 50 ml (1¾ fl oz/3½ tablespoons) water and mix well. Add the diced apricots and set aside.
- Combine the lemon juice and garlic paste for the creamy base layer and set aside.
- Place the cherry tomatoes over direct heat on the barbecue and cook for about 5 minutes until charred and soft.
- Drain the apricots and mix them with the remaining salsa ingredients and some salt and pepper.
- Whizz the drained sundried tomatoes with the harissa to a paste in a small blender and mix in the lemon juice.
- Combine the lemon juice and garlic mixture with the cream cheese and yoghurt and season with salt and pepper. Spread this mixture over a serving platter.
- Top with the charred tomatoes (pluck them from the vines, more or less), followed by the crumbled feta and the sundried tomato paste, then the apricot salsa, then drizzle over the tablespoon of pomegranate molasses to serve.

To cook indoors: Preheat a griddle pan over a high heat for at least 5 minutes. Char the tomatoes in it for 5 minutes, or until soft, wrinkled and charred in places.

Curried Crabby Nachos

Serves: 4, easily doubled
Prep: The crema and pickled onion can be prepared several hours in advance. Store the onions at room temperature and the crema in the fridge.
Cook and assembly time: 20 minutes

¼ red onion, finely chopped
2 tablespoons lime juice
½ teaspoon caster (superfine) sugar
1 × 170 g (6 oz) bag tortilla chips (or similar size)
¼ cucumber, deseeded and finely diced
1 fresh green or red chilli, thinly sliced
150 g (5½ oz) white crab meat
flaky sea salt

Curried crab crema
150 g (5½ oz/scant ⅔ cup) sour cream
1 teaspoon curry powder
1 tablespoon lime juice
50 g (1¾ oz) brown crab meat
a dash of smoky hot sauce, such as chipotle, to taste
flaky sea salt and ground white pepper

To serve
garam masala
handful of coriander (cilantro) leaves
lime wedges

This was born from the need to answer an important question: how can I combine crab and crisps on the same plate? These are show-off nachos, no doubt about it. But why not? Don't leave crab out in the blaring sunshine by the way, it's not up to it. This shouldn't be a problem though, because they won't last long.

● Combine the red onion with the lime juice, sugar and a generous couple of pinches of salt, toss to combine, then set aside.
● To make the crema, combine the sour cream, curry powder, lime juice, brown crab meat, hot sauce and some salt and white pepper in a bowl, mixing until smooth (you might need to mash the brown crab meat a bit with a fork).
● Spread a quarter of the crema across the base of 2 large serving platters and top each with tortilla chips. Divide the finely diced cucumber, drained pickled onions, chilli and white crab meat between them. Drizzle over the remaining crema, then top with a light dusting of garam masala and the coriander (cilantro) leaves. Serve with extra lime wedges.

Spicy Prawn Ceviche Cups

Serves: 4 as a starter, 8 as a nibble
Prep: The prawns (shrimp) can be deveined, diced and then stored in the fridge a couple of hours in advance. Don't marinate the ceviche for too long, as the lime juice will 'cook' the prawns too much and the dish will lose its freshness
Cook and assembly time: 30 minutes, including prawn deveining
Equipment: Cocktail stick, small blender, small paper cups or bowls

450 g (1 lb) raw king prawns (shrimp)
250 ml (8 fl oz/1 cup) lime juice
2 fresh green chillies
large handful of coriander (cilantro) leaves, chopped
20 small cherry tomatoes, quartered
½ small red onion, diced
1 tablespoon Tajin seasoning (or chilli powder)
2 ripe avocados, stoned, peeled and finely diced
½ cucumber, deseeded, peeled and finely diced
1 garlic clove, grated to a paste
generous pinch of flaky sea salt

There's something super slick about serving cups of ceviche – look at me with my confident seafood serve! This is full of electric flavours that ricochet around the palate, while the prawns (shrimp) remain plump and refreshing, just cooked by the lime juice. You want very fresh prawns from a fishmonger for this recipe, and I find the special trip part of the pleasure of prepping. Maximise their value by freezing the heads and shells for stock.

● Devein the prawns (shrimp) first. The easiest way to do this is using a cocktail stick. First, twist the head off the prawn, then peel off the body shell and legs. Hold the prawn up, the right way up, so that it's curled in a natural shape. Along the back of the prawn, you will see a black line – this is the intestinal tract. Insert the cocktail stick at the top of the prawn, skewering it widthways, and pull upwards until the tract comes out. You can then pull gently to remove it (there are plenty of videos online if this makes zero sense!). Give the prawns a rinse to ensure there's no remaining intestinal tract, then chop into evenly sized pieces (not too finely).
● Blend half the lime juice in a small blender with the green chillies and coriander (cilantro). Combine with the prawns and all the other ingredients, mix well and refrigerate for 20 minutes or up to 1 hour.
● Serve the ceviche in small paper cups or bowls.

Nibbles

Hildas (honey-roasted pineapple, ham and pickled chilli skewers)

Makes: about 30 hildas
Prep: The pineapple can be cooked a few hours in advance and served at room temperature. The hildas can be assembled an hour or so in advance
Cook and assembly time: 20 minutes
Equipment: Roasting dish, 30 cocktail sticks

Honey-roasted pineapple

1 pineapple, peeled, cored and cut into medium chunks
100 g (3½ oz) honey
½ teaspoon ground ginger
2 allspice berries, crushed
grated zest and juice of 1 lime
15 slices of Parma ham or another cured ham, cut in half to make 30 pieces
30 pickled chillies

These nibbles are a cross between the love-hate pizza topping (I love) and a Gilda, an iconic pintxos served in bars around the Basque Country. Usually made with olives, anchovies and pickled chillies, they're a classic. Annoy the Italians and the Spanish with just one plate of nibbles! I make no apologies.

● Prepare a barbecue for two-zone cooking as described on page 12.
● Place the pineapple chunks in a roasting dish. Combine the honey, ground ginger, crushed allspice, lime zest and juice and mix well. Pour this mixture over the pineapple and mix well. Place on the opposite side to the coals then close the lid and close the bottom and top vents three-quarters of the way. Cook for 10 minutes, then stir and cook for a further 10 minutes. Once roasted, remove from the barbecue and give it a good stir, then allow to cool.
● Once cool, skewer each piece of pineapple with a piece of ham and a pickled chilli.

To cook indoors: Roast the pineapple in an oven at 220°C (430°F/gas 9) for 20 minutes, stirring once.

Dips

Herb Garden Dip

Serves: 4, easily doubled
Prep: This is best made close to the time of serving, but an hour or so before won't hurt
Cook and assembly time: 5 minutes
Equipment: Small blender

handful of basil leaves
handful of tarragon leaves
handful of chives
handful of parsley
handful of mint leaves
1 Boursin garlic and herb cheese
4 tablespoons natural yoghurt
1 tablespoon lemon juice
1 scant teaspoon caster (superfine) sugar
flaky sea salt

Ideas for dipping
I always serve this with lots of crisp veggies including chicory (endive) and Little Gem (bibb lettuce) leaves, radishes, blanched asparagus if it's in season, blanched Tenderstem, sugar snaps, etc.

I don't actually have a herb garden (yet!) but this dip combines lots of different herbs so, you get the idea. It's a crowd-pleaser, and perfect when you want something full of fragrance and flavour but perhaps not cheesy or spicy (there are many recipes for cheesy and/or spicy dips elsewhere in this book, do not worry). I think that this works particularly well if you are serving something rich alongside it, like, for example, the Curried Crabby Nachos on page 76, because it will complement but not compete.

● Combine everything in a small blender and whizz until smooth.
● Season well with salt and serve with your chosen vegetables.

Dips

Whole Roasted Courgette, Feta, Honey and Mint Dip

Serves: 4, easily doubled
Prep: The dip can be made at least several hours in advance and then refrigerated until needed. Allow it to warm up to room temperature before serving, though
Cook and assembly time: 30 minutes
Equipment: Tongs, blender

2 courgettes (zucchini)
200 g (7 oz) block of feta
1 head of garlic
extra virgin olive oil, for drizzling
1 tablespoon pul biber or other mild chilli flakes (if using regular chilli flakes, reduce the quantity unless you want it really spicy)
1 tablespoon honey
grated zest of 1 lemon and juice of ½
handful of mint leaves
flaky sea salt and freshly ground black pepper

Ideas for dipping
tortilla chips or crisps
cucumber
seeded crackers
toasted pitta

This tastes of sunshine and Greek holidays, even if you've never had one to remember. I love roasting courgettes (zucchini) whole in the barbecue, and will often blacken them completely. For this, I've roasted them more gently and whizzed them into a simple yet super summery dip. If you're making the Hildas on page 80, you can cook this at the same time.

- Prepare a barbecue for two-zone cooking as described on page 12.
- Wrap the whole courgettes (zucchini) in foil, then place them directly onto the grill, away from the coals.
- Place the feta in a small baking dish. Add the head of garlic and drizzle the lot with olive oil. Sprinkle over the pul biber or chilli flakes and place this next to the courgettes.
- Close the lid, with the vents half closed, and bake for 20 minutes, or until the courgettes are soft when pricked with a fork and the feta and garlic are soft.
- Carefully unwrap the courgettes and add to a blender with the roasted garlic (the cloves squeezed out of their papery skins), feta, honey, lemon zest and juice, mint leaves and some black pepper. Whizz to a smooth paste. Make sure you season well again with salt and pepper.
- Decant into bowls and top each with a swirl of olive oil.

To cook indoors: Preheat the oven to 220°C (430°F/gas 9) and cook the wrapped courgettes, feta and garlic on a baking tray for the same amount of time as above.

Platters

Sticky Spiced Mango Pork Shoulder
with Mango Pickle

Serves: 4 with leftovers, or
8 people on the day
Prep: Make the mango pickle
a week in advance (you'll have
plenty of time to prep the rest
while the pork cooks)
Cook and assembly time:
6–8 hours
Equipment: Jar for the pickle,
temperature probe, heatproof
gloves, small blender

Pork shoulder

1 half pork shoulder (bone-in),
about 2.5 kg (5 lb 8 oz)
2 tablespoons hot paprika
100 g (3½ oz) mango chutney
grated zest of 1 lime
1 tablespoon onion powder
1 tablespoon garlic powder
2 tablespoons sea salt
a little neutral oil

Mustard mango pickle

1 teaspoon fenugreek seeds
3 tablespoons black
mustard seeds
4 unripe mangoes, peeled and
flesh diced into 2 cm (¾ inch)
cubes (you want 400 g/14 oz
mango flesh)
4 garlic cloves, crushed
2 tablespoons chilli powder
3 tablespoons vegetable or
groundnut oil
1 tablespoon flaky sea salt

Mango chutney-glazed pork, a homemade mango pickle and a mango barbecue sauce – if you don't like mango, I'd suggest choosing a different recipe. It's all piled into buns with Bombay mix, a fresh raita and herbs and it's the kind of pulled pork I'm here for – plenty of contrasting textures, lots of freshness to balance the sweet pork. The pickle here is based on classic Indian recipes, but I've used smaller pieces of slightly riper mango (rather than green) to speed up the pickling process.

The best option, if you are cooking in a regular kettle barbecue, is to find really good-quality charcoal briquettes, which do now exist. If you use high-quality lumpwood charcoal you are going to go through an awful lot of it over 6 hours. And if you use poor-quality charcoal, well, it's just going to taste awful.

It's nice to smoke the pork with some wood or chips, which you can buy online. Use a good all-rounder like oak, or try apple for something slightly more mellow. Really though, smoke is smoke.

● Toast the fenugreek seeds in a dry frying pan (skillet) over a medium heat until they smell fragrant, then set aside.
● Combine the mustard and fenugreek seeds in a spice grinder or pestle and mortar and give them just a quick pulse – you don't want a fine powder. Combine the mango, ground spices, crushed garlic, chilli powder, oil and salt in a bowl and mix well. Transfer to a sterilised jar, seal and set aside at room temperature for 24 hours. After this time, give it a stir, mixing every day for at least 5 days. After this time, any bitterness should subside, and it will start to taste incredible. Ensure everything is looking oily on top of the jar as this will keep the pickle fresh – add more oil if you need to.
● When you're ready to cook, trim the fat on the pork shoulder to a thickness of about 1 cm (½ inch) and remove any fibrous silverskin from the underside of the shoulder.
● Combine the paprika, mango chutney, lime zest, onion and garlic powders, salt and oil – you just want to add enough for the mixture to form a paste – and rub all over the pork shoulder.

Raita

1 cucumber, deseeded and diced
450 g (1 lb/2 cups) Greek
or natural yoghurt
squeeze of lime juice
flaky sea salt

Mango barbecue sauce

100 g (3½ oz) mustard mango
pickle (above)
25 ml (¾ fl oz/generous 1½
teaspoons) cider vinegar
1 tablespoon honey
or maple syrup
1 tablespoon ketchup
½ teaspoon onion powder
½ teaspoon garlic powder
1 teaspoon hot paprika
½ tablespoon soft dark
brown sugar
1 teaspoon Worcestershire sauce

To serve

white buns
Bombay mix
coriander (cilantro) leaves
mint leaves
thinly sliced red onion

● Prepare a barbecue for two-zone cooking as described on page 12, with the lit coals on one side (add a chunk of wood if you have one) and a tray to catch drips on the other. Check the charcoal now and then, topping up if needed. There's no point adding more wood after a couple of hours – the pork is smoked. Close the lid and set both vents to a quarter open.

● The total cooking time is likely to be 6–8 hours. At some point, the temperature of the meat will stop rising – this is called a 'stall'. It might happen at about 65–75°C (150–167°F). At this point, wrap it in layers of foil and return it to the barbecue.

● Continue cooking for another few hours until the internal temperature of the pork reaches 90°C (194°F) before removing from the heat, to ensure the connective tissue has melted down. Set the pork aside to rest, wrapped, for at least 30 minutes.

● Toss the diced cucumber with a generous pinch of salt and place into a colander over a bowl to drain.

● In a small blender, combine all the barbecue sauce ingredients until smooth.

● Drain and rinse the cucumber and mix with the other raita ingredients. Season with salt and pepper.

● Once the meat has rested, pull it apart over a tray to catch any juices, taking care to remove any small, sharp bones. Don't over-pull – you want to leave some nice big chunks of meat.

● Toss the meat with 50 ml (1¾ fl oz/3½ tablespoons) or so of the fatty juices and some salt, plus as much as the barbecue sauce as you like – it's better to be a little cautious and serve the rest on the side. Serve the pork with buns, raita, mango pickle and garnishes.

To cook indoors: Preheat the oven to 130°C (260°F/gas 2). Place the mango-coated pork on a rack in a roasting tin and pour 500 ml (17 fl oz/generous 2 cups) water into the bottom of the tray (avoiding the pork). Cover tightly with foil and cook for anything between 6 and 8 hours, or until falling apart.

Platters

Charred Onion-Chermoula Prawns
with 'Nduja, Ricotta and Fennel Butter Cornbread

Serves: 8, prawns (shrimp) and chermoula recipe easily scaled down to serve 4 with leftover cornbread
Prep: The chermoula can be made several hours in advance
Cook and assembly time: 1 hour
Equipment: Cast-iron skillet or similar heatproof pan for the cornbread, kitchen scissors, small blender, heatproof gloves

32 large shell-on prawns (shrimp) (4 prawns per person)
neutral oil, for grilling
sea salt and freshly ground black pepper

Charred onion chermoula
6 spring onions (scallions)
15 g (½ oz) dill
20 g (¾ oz) basil
15 g (½ oz) coriander (cilantro)
10 g (¼ oz) mint
½ preserved lemon, rind only
2 garlic cloves
1 teaspoon cumin seeds, toasted
1 teaspoon sweet paprika
or pul biber
150 ml (5 fl oz/⅔ cup) extra virgin olive oil
2–3 tablespoons lemon juice

I'm in love with grilled prawns (shrimp) – plump pink commas with whiskers that crackle and curl. I also adore the messy business of eating them – to me, one of the best things about a barbecue is the lack of stiffness around diving in with your hands. I snip the prawns through their shells to butterfly them, which means the shell protects them on the grill, they look beautiful, and I'm guaranteed easy access to the meat within, plus all the fun of sucking their casings clean. Here I've dressed them with a sparkly green chermoula, heady with herbs and an ideal match for the frankly outrageous cornbread, which has pockets of fluffy ricotta, scarlet 'nduja and a liberal soaking of fennel seed butter.

- Prepare a barbecue for two-zone cooking as described on page 12.
- Prepare the prawns (shrimp) by laying them on their backs and cutting up through their legs and bellies to butterfly them. Remove any intestinal tracts, which should be easy to find once they're butterflied. Chill.
- Combine the cornmeal, flour, bicarbonate of soda (baking soda), baking powder and salt in a large bowl.
- In a separate bowl, combine the milk, honey, eggs, half the 'nduja (in nuggets is fine) and sweetcorn. Make a well in the centre of the dry ingredients, add the milk mixture and whisk to make a batter.
- Once the barbecue is ready, toss the spring onions (scallions) with a little neutral oil and place over direct heat. Cook for about 5 minutes until lightly charred all over.
- Place the skillet over direct heat too and add the oil.
- Once it starts to sizzle, pour in the batter and drop the ricotta in blobs on top. Cook for 5–10 minutes, or until you can see the cornbread is beginning to cook around the sides.
- Move the cornbread over to indirect heat, close the lid and half-close the vents and cook for a further 15–20 minutes or until a skewer inserted into the middle comes out clean.

'Nduja and ricotta cornbread

150 g (5½ oz/scant 1 cup)
coarse cornmeal
150 g (5½ oz/1¼ cups) plain
(all-purpose) flour
1 teaspoon bicarbonate of soda
(baking soda)
1 teaspoon baking powder
2 teaspoons flaky sea salt
240 ml (8 fl oz/1 cup)
whole (full-fat) milk
2 tablespoons honey
2 eggs
100 g (3½ oz) 'nduja, plus
1 tablespoon for melting
165 g (5¾ oz) sweetcorn
(drained weight of a small tin)
2 tablespoons neutral oil
100 g (3½ oz/scant ½ cup) ricotta

Fennel butter

50 g (1¾ oz/3½ tablespoons)
butter
1 tablespoon honey, plus extra to
serve, if you like
1 teaspoon fennel seeds

● Combine the charred spring onions and all the other chermoula ingredients and some salt in a small blender and whizz to a paste.

● Carefully remove the cornbread from the grill using heatproof gloves. Combine the butter, 'nduja, honey and fennel seeds in a pan until melted. Poke holes all over the cornbread using a skewer, then pour over the butter, spreading it evenly.

● While the cornbread cools, toss the prawns with a little neutral oil and cook over direct heat for a minute on each side, or until pink.

● Serve the prawns on a plate topped with the chermoula, and the cornbread on the side.

Platters

Grilled Bavette (or Portobellos)
with Sour Creamed Corn and Lime Pickle Butter

Serves: 4, easily doubled
Prep: The creamed corn and lime butter can be made at least a few hours in advance. Gently reheat the creamed corn before serving
Cook and assembly time: 30 minutes for the steak/mushrooms and corn
Equipment: Tongs, stick blender

---

2 × bavette steaks weighing about 200 g (7 oz) each, or 4 portobello mushrooms, stems trimmed
neutral oil, for cooking
handful of coriander (cilantro) leaves
flaky sea salt and freshly ground black pepper

Sour creamed corn
dash of neutral oil
120 g (4¼ oz/9 tablespoons) butter
1 onion, finely chopped
1 × 340 g (12 oz) tin sweetcorn, drained
120 ml (4 fl oz/½ cup) single (light) cream

Lime pickle butter
2 teaspoons lime pickle, finely chopped
50 g (1¾ oz/3½ tablespoons) butter, softened so it's mashable

Bavette is one of my all-time favourite cuts of steak because it cooks super fast, is relatively affordable and packed with flavour. It's crucial that you sear it quickly then let it rest well before slicing thinly against the grain. Do all that, and you'll never look back.

There are a few elements here, but of course you could make the steak/mushrooms and corn without the potatoes on page 95, and vice versa. It's your party!

● Prepare a barbecue for two-zone cooking as described on page 12.
● To cook the onion for the creamed corn, heat the oil and butter in a frying pan (skillet) over a medium heat, add the onion and soften gently for about 10 minutes.
● While the onion's softening, cook the steaks. Rub them with a little oil, season them really well with sea salt and place directly over the coals. Cook for a few minutes on each side – exact cooking times will depend on the thickness of the steak. A thicker piece might take 4–5 minutes on each side. Set aside to rest.
● If using mushrooms, brush them with oil and season with salt, grill gill-side down for about 5 minutes, then flip and cook for a further few minutes, or until tender.
● Add 50 ml (1¾ fl oz/3½ tablespoons) water to the onion along with the corn, then turn down the heat to low and cook gently for 10 minutes. Add the cream and season, then simmer for 1 minute. Purée half of the creamed corn – this is easiest using a stick/hand blender – then combine it with the unblended corn.
● To make the lime pickle butter, place the butter in a small saucepan and cook over a medium-low heat until it begins to turn brown and nutty, then add the lime pickle. Mix well to combine.
● Slice the steak or mushrooms thinly and serve on top of the creamed corn. Top with brown butter and coriander (cilantro).

To cook indoors: Preheat a griddle pan over a high heat for at least 5 minutes. Cook the steaks or mushrooms as above.

Sides

Tomato Salad
with Sizzled Ginger Dressing

Serves: 4, easily doubled
Prep: Best made just before
serving
Cook and assembly time:
15 minutes

450 g (1 lb) ripe tomatoes, sliced

Sizzled ginger dressing
1 tablespoon coconut oil
2 garlic cloves, thinly sliced
1 thumb of ginger, peeled (use a
teaspoon for ease) and sliced into
matchstick-shaped pieces
1 tablespoon fish sauce
1 tablespoon caster (superfine)
sugar
1 fresh green chilli, thinly sliced
handful of coriander (cilantro),
leaves picked and stalks
finely chopped
2 tablespoons lime juice
flaky sea salt

It's no exaggeration to say that I eat tomatoes every day through summer. A bowl of cherry tomatoes lives on my desk and I eat larger ones sliced and dressed simply with olive oil, vinegar, salt and basil. However, it's fun to push things slightly further for a party. While this dish is very easy to put together, it's showing off bold flavours including matchsticks of ginger, frazzled in coconut oil. Never underestimate the power of fish sauce as a general seasoning, either. I use it in so many dishes, as you'll notice as you browse through this book.

● Heat the coconut oil in a small saucepan over a medium heat. Add the garlic and ginger and reduce the heat to low, letting it sizzle for up to 5 minutes, or until the garlic and ginger are lightly golden.
● Stir in the fish sauce, sugar, green chilli and coriander (cilantro) stalks, stirring until the sugar is dissolved.
● Remove from the heat and add a pinch of salt and the lime juice.
● Arrange the tomatoes on a serving plate and pour over the dressing. Top with the coriander leaves.

Sides

Panch Phoron Potato Salad

Serves: 4, easily doubled
Prep: Potatoes can be par-boiled a few hours in advance and panch phoron made up to a week in advance and stored in an airtight container.
Cook and assembly time: 30 minutes

400 g (14 oz) new potatoes
neutral oil, for cooking
125 g (4½ oz/½ cup) natural yoghurt
50 g (1¾ oz/3½ tablespoons) unsalted butter
1 fresh green chilli, thinly sliced
flaky sea salt, for sprinkling

Panch phoron
1 tablespoon brown mustard seeds
1 tablespoon fennel seeds
1 tablespoon fenugreek seeds
1 tablespoon nigella seeds
1 tablespoon cumin seeds

Panch phoron is a spice blend used across Eastern and Northeastern India. I love to use it in a potato salad as the spices are crushed lightly, which means you get little nuggets of flavour flecked throughout.

● If you're grilling the potatoes, prepare a barbecue for direct cooking over a medium-high heat.
● Par-cook the new potatoes in salted boiling water for 5 minutes, then drain.
● Combine the panch phoron spices in a small frying pan (skillet) over a medium heat and toast for a few minutes, stirring them regularly, until fragrant. Remove and crush lightly using a pestle and mortar then set aside.
● Coat the potatoes with a little neutral oil, then transfer to the grill. Cook the potatoes over direct heat, turning them regularly, until crisp and charred on the outside and tender all the way through.
● Spread the yoghurt over a serving platter and season with flaky sea salt.
● Combine the butter and sliced green chilli in a small saucepan and cook gently until the butter has melted and the chilli is sizzling.
● Crush each potato lightly with a fork then place on top of the yoghurt. Pour over the chilli butter, garnish liberally with panch phoron and finish with a final sprinkle of flaky sea salt.

To cook indoors: Cook the potatoes fully in salted boiling water for 10–15 minutes.

Sides

Grilled and Chilled Peppers
in Harissa, Pineapple and Honey

Serves: 6
Prep: Make this one a couple of hours in advance, so it has time to chill
Cook and assembly time: 30 minutes

6 red, yellow or orange (bell) peppers (or a mix of all three)
300 ml (10 fl oz/1¼ cups) pineapple juice
1 tablespoon honey
1 tablespoon harissa
2 tablespoons lime juice
flaky sea salt
basil leaves, to garnish

An elegant do-ahead side, this. It's so simple yet will garner many compliments, I promise. A chilled dish feels like a very slick move, too – a way to appear like the effortless host. There are so few ingredients, but the result really sings.

● Prepare a barbecue for two-zone cooking as described on page 12.
● Place the peppers directly over the coals and cook them for about 10 minutes until blackened on all sides.
● Transfer to a bowl and cover the bowl tightly with cling film (plastic wrap) then allow to sit for 10 minutes more – this will allow them to soften completely inside and make the skins easier to remove.
● Combine the pineapple juice and honey in a small saucepan then bring to a simmer and reduce by half, until syrupy. Stir in the harissa and lime juice and season with salt.
● Remove the pepper skins by slipping them off with your fingers (this is easy to do under a running tap) and remove the seeds and stalks. Don't worry if some black parts remain as these will add to the flavour. Thickly slice the peppers and transfer to a bowl.
● Mix the peppers with the dressing, allow to cool, then chill until needed. Arrange the peppers for everyone to help themselves and garnish with basil.

Sides

Gem Salad
with Secret Weapon Dressing

Serves: 4–6
Prep time: Make the dressing
a few hours in advance if you like,
but don't dress the salad until
you're ready to serve
Assembly time: 10 minutes
Equipment: Small blender

3 gem lettuces, leaves
separated
1 cucumber, sliced

Secret weapon dressing
1 tablespoon fish sauce
handful of basil
handful of chives
2 spring onions (scallions),
trimmed
1 ripe avocado, stoned
and peeled
2 garlic cloves, peeled
3 tablespoons natural yoghurt
2 tablespoons white wine vinegar
(or cider vinegar, or lemon juice)
3 tablespoons extra virgin olive oil
1 fresh green chilli
pinch of flaky sea salt

Here's a salad dressing that will never let you down. It's creamy with avocado and yoghurt, savoury with fish sauce and really fresh with lots of herbs. It clings to salad like a limpet to a rock and it's also fabulous as a dip or a sauce for grilled meat, fish or veg. You're welcome.

Sometimes I'll add cooked Tenderstem broccoli to this salad, or you could do a charred green salad with quartered little gem and sugar snaps. I've kept it simple for this recipe, but you get the idea: she's got your back.

● Blend all the dressing ingredients together in a small blender. It should be bright and acidic but also creamy, herbal and salty. It's not a demure dressing and that is the point. If it's very thick, loosen it cautiously with a small splash of water.
● Wash and dry the salad leaves properly using a salad spinner or kitchen paper. Toss with the cucumber and the dressing before dividing between serving plates.

Tequila-macerated Strawberries
with Salted Whipped Cream

Serves: 4, easily doubled
Prep: Marinate the strawberries
for at least 30 minutes – I like to
leave them for the duration
of the meal
Assembly time: See above – this
takes moments of hands-on time
Equipment: Whisk

500 g (1 lb 2 oz) fresh
strawberries, hulled and
quartered
50 ml (1¾ fl oz/3½ tablespoons)
tequila
50 g (1¾ oz/¼ cup) caster
(superfine) sugar
50 ml (1¾ fl oz/3½ tablespoons)
lime juice

Salted whipped cream
150 ml (5 fl oz/⅔ cup)
whipping cream
½ teaspoon flaky sea salt
2 teaspoons caster
(superfine) sugar

This may just be the best last-minute dessert to have in your back pocket. Macerating the strawberries intensifies their sweetness, and the tequila flavour is a bonus. A scoop of lightly salted whipped cream on top and you will have served something a bit clever, definitely elegant and, most importantly, really delicious with barely any effort.

● Mix the strawberries with the tequila, sugar and lime juice and let them stand while you enjoy your meal (or for at least 30 minutes). Stir them occasionally.
● To serve, whip the cream with the salt and sugar to soft peaks – the key to softly whipped cream is stopping before you think it's done.
● Serve the strawberries with a dollop of the salted cream.

Lemon, Jalapeño and Lemongrass Granita

Serves: 4, easily doubled
Prep: Make this at least 5 hours in advance as freezers can vary quite a bit, despite claiming to be the same temperature. It may well be done after 3 hours, but could take 5.
Cook and assembly time: 30 minutes
Equipment: Shallow tray or dish for freezing the granita, sieve

grated zest of 3 lemons
250 ml (8 fl oz/1 cup) fresh lemon juice (you're going to need about 16 lemons in total)
125 g (4½ oz/¾ cup) caster (superfine) sugar
250 ml (8 fl oz/1 cup) water
1 fresh green chilli or jalapeño, slit lengthways
2 lemongrass stalks, bruised
3 tablespoons vodka

This is one of the most supremely refreshing and delicious things you can eat on a hot day, and it's amazing how the steeping brings out the flavour of the jalapeño, without the heat. The vodka in the mixture stops this freezing solid and results in a smoother granita. I've also served this with a shot of vodka on top before, depending on how the party is going...

If you want to make the punch on page 27, make a double quantity of the syrup below – two birds, one stone.

● If you want to serve the granita in lemon halves, make sure to cut 4 (or however many you need) of the lemons lengthways when you juice them. Juice the lemons then reform them into lemon half shapes and place into the freezer so that they will be cold to receive the granita later.
● Combine the sugar and water in a saucepan and bring to the boil, stirring to dissolve the sugar. Add the zest, juice, chilli, lemongrass and vodka to the syrup and set aside to cool. Transfer to the fridge and chill for 1 hour.
● Strain the syrup, then transfer to a shallow tray and freeze for 45 minutes, then remove from the freezer and give it a good stir, especially around the edges. Do this a couple more times, every 40 minutes, until it's frozen into a granita.
● About 20 minutes before you're ready to serve, remove the granita from the freezer to allow it to soften a little (it might not need this, but just in case) then pile into bowls or the lemon halves.

Desserts

No-churn Vietnamese Coffee Ice Cream

Serves: 10
Prep: Needs to freeze overnight
Cook and assembly time:
10 minutes
Equipment: Large freezerproof
tub, electric whisk

---

600 ml (20 fl oz/2½ cups)
whipping cream
1 × 397 g (14 oz) tin
condensed milk
2 tablespoons ground
espresso coffee
2 tablespoons Baileys
pinch of flaky sea salt

Yes, there is a way to make ice cream without an ice-cream maker, and no, you don't need to take it out of the freezer every hour to do any furious mixing (you do still need to freeze it, I'm afraid...). The key to a no-churn ice cream is condensed milk, but I've always found the flavour a little jarring – just that bit too distinct from the regular, custard-based stuff. Until I had a thought: why not make a frozen version of something that already includes condensed milk as an ingredient? Hello, Vietnamese iced coffee, that beautifully sweet, thick and – crucially – cold caffeinated drink.

You could also add some chocolate chips into the mix, if that's your thing. Personally, I love a slosh of Baileys. Your ice cream may be visibly flecked, depending on the coffee you use – this is fine.

● Line a large freezerproof tub with cling film (plastic wrap) (this isn't necessary but it's much easier to get it out when it's finished, plus the overhang protects the top from forming ice crystals).
● Using an electric whisk, whip everything together until you have soft peaks – it should resemble clotted cream, with a slightly lighter texture.
● Transfer to the tub, then fold the cling film over the top. Put the lid on and transfer to the freezer overnight (although it should be ready after about 6 hours). Depending on the enthusiasm of your freezer, you may need to let the ice cream soften a little before scooping.

Autu

Leaves rustle, logs crackle,
charcoal glows to life.
Coals tinkle through
the keen autumn air –
a thousand tiny bells.
Hands clasped around
a steaming brew, the grill
is set for smoked soup,
slow-roasted wings.
As nights draw in I relish
these moments, a transition
to a different rhythm –
smoking and roasting over
hot, fast grilling. I invite
people over for a first-days-
of-autumn feast – silky
aubergines, sticky smothered
lamb and ice cream with
coal-toasted meringues.

Menus

Today

Autumn

Drinks
Honeydew and Jalapeño Sours

Nibbles
Salami, Pickled Onion and Parmesan Twists
with Dill (AKA Holly's Pastries)

Dip
Yoghurt, Sriracha Brown-buttered Corn
and 'Nduja Crumbs

Platter
Super Herbal Chicken Wings

Side
Soy Buttered Potatoes

Dessert
Grilled Plums, Five-spice Crumble and
Honey-Rum Cream

Tomorrow

Next week

Drinks
Smoky Peach Iced Tea

Drinks
Fermented Tomato and Gochujang
Bloody Marys

Nibbles
Advanced Player Barbecued Garlic Bread

Nibbles
Anchovies with Burnt Shallot Butter

Dip
Smoky Aubergine, Maple-pickled Sultanas
and Garam Masala Onions

Dip
Skillet Focaccia with Artichoke Dip

Platter
Sticky Scotch Bonnet and Citrus-smothered
Lamb with Confit Garlic and Peppers

Platter
Spice-smothered Hasselback Squash (or Lamb
Chops) with Ricotta and Green Chilli Sauce

Side
Herbal Cabbage Salad with Avocado Cream

Side
Dreamy, Creamy White Beans with
Confit Garlic

Dessert
Chilled 'n' Boozy Chocolate 'Cake' with
Sherbety Cherries

Dessert
Burnt Meringue, Vanilla Ice Cream and
Olive Oil

Honeydew and Jalapeño Sours

Makes: 4
Prep: The simple syrup can
be made a few days in advance
and refrigerated.
Cook and mixing time: 15 minutes
Equipment: Small blender, sieve,
cocktail shaker, strainer
Glass: Short, like an Old
Fashioned

---

100 ml (3½ fl oz/scant ½ cup) pisco
50 ml (1¾ fl oz/3½ tablespoons)
mezcal
100 ml (3½ fl oz/scant ½ cup)
lime juice
400 ml (14 fl oz/generous 1½ cups)
melon and jalapeño juice (below)
100 ml (3½ fl oz/scant ½ cup)
simple syrup (below)
2 egg whites
angostura bitters
ice cubes

Simple syrup
100 g (3½ oz/scant ½ cup) caster
(superfine) sugar
100 ml (3½ fl oz/scant ½ cup)
water

Melon and jalapeño juice
1 honeydew melon (about 1 kg/
2 lb 4 oz), seeds removed and
flesh diced
1 fresh jalapeño, stalk removed
250 ml (8 fl oz/1 cup) water
handful of mint leaves

Rim
flaky sea salt
lime wedge

Combining jalapeño with the heady, candied musk of
melon serves to reveal the chilli's fruity perfume. Find the ripest
melon you can for this recipe. To test it, press your thumb into
the end opposite the stem – if there is a slight give, the odds
are in your favour.

I love both the body and froth of a sour, which come from
the egg white, plus it feels a little sophisticated – like you've made
a 'proper cocktail'.

● Make the simple syrup by combining the sugar and water in
a saucepan and heating gently until the sugar has dissolved.
Allow to cool before using (do this over a bowl of ice if you're
in a hurry).
● Combine the melon, jalapeño, water and mint in a small
blender and whizz until smooth, then pass through a sieve
to remove the pulp, pressing down to extract all the juice.
You should have about 500 ml (17 fl oz/generous 2 cups).
● Dust a plate with flaky sea salt. Run the lime wedge around
the rims of the glasses, then dip them into the salt. If you have
room, pop the glasses into the freezer.
● You will need to make the cocktails in two batches, so combine
half the pisco, mezcal, lime juice, melon and jalapeño juice,
100 ml (3½ fl oz/scant ½ cup) simple syrup and 1 egg white
in a cocktail shaker with a dash of angostura bitters and shake
for 10 seconds.
● Add ice and shake the shaker vigorously until it's really cold.
Strain through the Hawthorne strainer into the cold glasses,
over ice. Repeat with the second half of the ingredients.

Drinks

Fermented Tomato and Gochujang Bloody Marys

Makes: 4
Assembly time: 15 minutes, plus
1 week fermentation time
Equipment: Sterilised 1 litre
(34 fl oz) jar, blender, sieve,
cocktail sticks
Glass: Tall, like a Collins glass

1 tablespoon Worcestershire
sauce
1 tablespoon gochujang
500 ml (17 fl oz/generous 2 cups)
fermented tomato and celery
juice (below)
200 ml (7 fl oz/scant 1 cup) vodka

**Fermented tomatoes
and celery**
1 kg (2 lb 4 oz) cherry tomatoes,
stems removed and washed
50 g (1¾ oz) flaky sea salt
1 litre (34 fl oz/4½ cups) water
200 g (7 oz) celery, washed,
strings removed and stalks
cut into short lengths
½ head of garlic, cloves separated
and peeled
2 fresh red chillies, sliced
½ teaspoon black peppercorns

To serve
ice cubes
8 silverskin onions
8 cornichons
celery sticks

For me, a great Bloody Mary has waspish intensity. I want people to take a sip and smack their lips with satisfaction. The drink should let you know who's boss, yet glide down far too easily. I achieve this using fermentation – tomatoes and celery are brined with black peppercorns, then blended into a precious juice, while gochujang adds sweet heat. I never serve these without the garnish of pickles and *plenty* of ice. For me, the drink works at any time of day (within reason), but the juice alone is fantastic at breakfast time.

● Prick each cherry tomato with the end of a sharp knife or a cocktail stick.
● Dissolve the salt in the water by combining both in a jug and stirring until the salt has dissolved.
● Place the tomatoes and celery in the sterilised jar with the garlic cloves, chillies and peppercorns. Pour in the brine.
● Weigh everything down with something like a small dish or a sealable sandwich bag filled with water, then close the lid. Allow to ferment for a week at room temperature, ensuring you burp the jar every day (open the lid to allow gas to escape).
● After 1 week, strain the ferment over a bowl, reserving the tomatoes, celery, garlic, and the brine.
● Place the tomatoes, chillies, celery and garlic into a blender with 100 ml (3½ fl oz/scant ½ cup) of the brine and whizz to a paste. Strain through a sieve, pressing to extract all the juice. This should make about 500 ml (17 fl oz/generous 2 cups) juice. If it doesn't, return the mash to the blender with a splash of the juice and blend and pass again.
● Fill 4 glasses and a jug with ice.
● Mix the Worcestershire sauce and gochujang until smooth.
● In the jug, combine the tomato and celery juice, vodka and the gochujang mixture and stir well, then pour into the glasses.
● Thread the onions and cornichons onto cocktail sticks. Finish the drinks with the celery sticks and onions/cornichons and serve.

Drinks

Smoky Peach Iced Tea

Makes: 4
Prep time: Chilling time for the
tea and fruit
Cook and mixing time: 10 minutes
Equipment: Potato masher, sieve
Glass: Short, like an
Old Fashioned

2 ripe peaches, stoned
and roughly chopped
125 g (4½ oz/generous ½ cup)
caster (superfine) sugar
250 ml (8 fl oz/1 cup) water
2 teaspoons lapsang souchong
tea leaves
ice cubes
shot of bourbon per glass
squeeze of lemon juice

I adore peach iced tea when stone fruits are at their ripest and, of course, it begs for booze. I use lapsang souchong to add a smoky element, too; it's a black tea that's smoked over pinewood, and it's perfect with the summer-meets-autumn, almost festering ripeness of the fruit. The tea needs to be chilled after brewing, but this can be done quickly by pouring it into a bowl set inside a larger bowl of iced water.

● Combine the peaches, sugar and water in a saucepan, bring to a simmer and cook until the sugar has dissolved.
● Mash the peaches with a potato masher. Turn off the heat, put a lid on and leave to infuse for 30 minutes, then strain through a sieve into a bowl, pushing down on the flesh to extract all the flavour. Chill the syrup.
● Brew the tea leaves with 600 ml (20 fl oz/2½ cups) boiling water for a few minutes, then strain and chill that too.
● Fill all the glasses with ice, then add a shot of bourbon to each, along with 50–100 ml (1¾ fl oz/3½ tablespoons–3½ fl oz/scant ½ cup) of the peach syrup (it's best to start with a little bit, then increase to your taste). Top up with the chilled tea, then add a small squeeze of lemon juice, stir and serve.

Nibbles

Salami, Pickled Onion and Parmesan Twists with Dill
(AKA Holly's Pastries)

Makes: 16 (quantities easily halved)
Prep: Best made and eaten close to serving, but making them a couple of hours ahead won't hurt
Cook and assembly time: 40 minutes
Equipment: Pastry brush

2 sheets of ready-rolled puff pastry
a little flour, for dusting
200 g (7 oz) Parmesan cheese, grated
150 g (5½ oz) salami, finely chopped
50 pickled silverskin onions, finely chopped

Dill glaze
large bunch of dill, finely chopped
2 tablespoons runny honey
100 g (3½ oz/7 tablespoons) butter, melted
2 tablespoons lemon juice

Holly Catford (best friend, creative partner and designer of this book) has a hardcore love of pastries and dill, so you can see how this happened. I did question whether or not I should include a pastry recipe in a barbecue book but then I thought, why not? They're a top-tier nibble that works particularly well with the Honeydew and Jalapeño Sours on page 112.

● Preheat the oven to 210°C (410°F/gas 7) and line a baking sheet with baking paper.
● Lay out a puff pastry sheet on a lightly floured surface.
● Sprinkle over half the Parmesan, then the salami and pickled onions, then the remaining Parmesan.
● Cut the pastry into 8 strips using a knife or a pizza wheel, then place the second sheet of pastry on top.
● Pick up each strip at either end and twist, until the length of the pastry is twisted, then place on the lined baking sheet and bake in the oven for 30 minutes, or until golden brown.
● Combine the glaze ingredients in a bowl and mix well.
● Remove from the oven, and while they're still hot, use a pastry brush to glaze each twist generously, making sure each is covered with plenty of dill.
● Let them cool, then cut each twist in half to make 16 (if you do this before they're cooked, they will unravel in the oven).

Nibbles

Advanced Player
Barbecued Garlic Bread

Serves: 8 (2 wedges per person)
Prep: The bread can be prepped
a few hours before cooking and
wrapped ready to heat on the
barbecue or in the oven.
Cook and assembly time:
40 minutes
Equipment: Baking tray, foil,
pastry brush

1 whole, round or oval
farmhouse-style white loaf
250 g (9 oz/generous 1 cup)
cream cheese
bunch of chives, finely chopped
grated zest of 1 lemon
flaky sea salt and freshly ground
black pepper

Garlic butter
200 g (7 oz/14 tablespoons)
salted butter, melted
1 head of garlic, cloves peeled
and crushed or finely grated
handful of parsley leaves,
finely chopped
2 tablespoons grated
Parmesan cheese
1 tablespoon honey
1 egg, lightly beaten
50 ml (1¾ fl oz/3½ tablespoons)
milk

This is a mashup of Korean and European-style garlic breads.
The Korean style uses cream cheese and egg, which brings
a slightly wobbly, custardy quality to the centre, while the crust
becomes burnished bronze. It works well for any occasion –
obviously, it's garlic bread – but I love it when there's a nip
in the air and people are craving something comforting.
It's also a reliable end of evening soaker-upper. One thing to
note: it's likely to be the most garlicky garlic bread you've ever
tasted in your entire garlic bread career. Advanced players only.

● Use a bread knife to slice across the loaf in a star shape,
making 8 cuts so that you end up with 16 wedges, making sure
not to cut through the base of the loaf.
● Prepare a barbecue for two-zone cooking as described
on page 12.
● Mix together the cheese, chives and lemon zest in a bowl. Add
some salt and pepper and spread the mixture inside the wedges.
● To make the garlic butter, combine the melted butter, crushed or
grated garlic, parsley, Parmesan, honey, egg and milk and season
with black pepper.
● Brush the garlic butter all over the loaf and into all the gaps
using a pastry brush. I usually do this as much as possible,
then just pour the remainder into the cracks.
● Wrap the whole loaf really well in foil. Place the wrapped loaf
onto a baking tray and warm it over indirect heat for 35 minutes
with the lid closed and bottom vents half closed, turning the
bread around once, to make sure it's evenly cooked.
● Carefully peel back the foil and return to the barbecue for
a couple of minutes, or until crisp on the outside. It will still be
soft and custardy in the middle, but you want a nice contrast
with the crackly outside.

To cook indoors: Place in the centre of the oven at 200°C
(400°F/gas 6) for 45 minutes, unwrapping at the end as above.

Nibbles

Anchovies
with Burnt Shallot Butter

Serves: 4, with lots of leftover butter, or of course you could scale it up or down
Prep: The butter can be made a day or so in advance and refrigerated.
Cook and assembly time: 30 minutes
Equipment: Tongs, small blender

4–6 banana shallots
250 g (9 oz/15 tablespoons) butter
1 × 47 g (1½ oz) tin good-quality anchovies in oil

To serve
lemon wedges
bread (either chunks of the Skillet Focaccia on page 124, or your choice of something sturdy in texture)

You need to really burn the s**t out of the shallots here – the skins should be totally black and the insides soft and buttery. Blended with butter and eaten with the saline sting of anchovy they are pure magic. I love to serve this with chunks of the focaccia on page 124.

● Prepare a barbecue for two-zone cooking as described on page 12.
● Place the unpeeled shallots over direct heat and cook for about 20 minutes until totally blackened all over, turning them with tongs occasionally. Check they're soft in the centre before removing and, if not, move them to indirect heat to finish cooking through.
● Place the butter in a small blender then squeeze out the soft innards of the shallots. Crumble in some of the burnt skin too, to really get the burnt flavour. Whizz to combine.
● Serve the elements separately, draining the anchovies, so people can choose their own adventure.

Skillet Focaccia
with Artichoke Dip

Serves: Focaccia serves 8–10, dip serves 4–6
Prep: The bread is best eaten on the day it's made. The dip can be made a few hours in advance and chilled, but should come to room temperature before serving.
Cook and assembly time: 30 minutes, plus 6 hours rising time
Equipment: Dough scraper, cast-iron frying pan (skillet), heatproof gloves, small blender

2 × 7 g sachets fast-action dried yeast
2 teaspoons caster (superfine) sugar
480 ml (16 fl oz/2 cups) lukewarm water
600 g (1 lb 5 oz/4¾ cups) plain (all-purpose) flour
1 tablespoon flaky sea salt, plus extra for the top
9 tablespoons extra virgin olive oil
needles from 1 large sprig of rosemary

Artichoke dip
1 × 280 g (9¾ oz) jar artichokes in oil, drained
1 garlic clove
250 g (9 oz/generous 1 cup) cream cheese
4 tablespoons olive oil
6 tablespoons sour cream, crème fraîche or yoghurt
handful of mint leaves
small handful of chives
1 tablespoon lemon juice

This focaccia is a real confidence booster; easy to make and guaranteed to emerge looking proudly dramatic, glistening and crackling with a dark, undulating crust.

● Combine the yeast with the sugar and water and whisk to combine. Set aside for 5 minutes – it should become frothy.
● Add the flour and salt and mix to combine until you have a dough. It will be really sticky and shaggy looking. Use a dough scraper to pick it up off the work surface, or a spatula.
● Add a couple of tablespoons of the olive oil to a really large bowl and tip the dough into it, turning it over to coat.
● Allow to rise at room temperature for 2–3 hours, or until doubled in size. It should be really bubbly and jiggly.
● Grease a cast-iron frying pan (skillet) with another few tablespoons of the olive oil.
● Oil your hands and bring the dough up and over itself into the centre of the bowl 4 times, making a quarter turn each time, then turn the dough out into the skillet, seam-side down.
● Allow to rise again at room temperature for a further 1–3 hours, or until doubled in size again.
● When you're ready to cook, prepare a barbecue for two-zone cooking as described on page 12, with high heat, and whizz the dip ingredients in a small blender.
● Oil your hands really well, then make deep dimples in the dough with your fingers, pressing right down to the bottom of the pan. Cover really well with an extra few tablespoons of olive oil, then sprinkle generously with sea salt and rosemary.
● Place the pan over indirect heat with the lid closed and the vents half closed top and bottom and cook for 20–25 minutes or until dark brown on top. Remove from the heat and let the bread cool a little before serving with the dip alongside.

To cook indoors: Preheat the oven to 260°C (500°F/gas 9) and bake for 25–30 minutes.

Dips

Smoky Aubergine
Maple-pickled Sultanas
and Garam Masala Onions

Serves: 4
Cook and assembly time: 1 hour
(the sultanas can be pickled up
to a week ahead, and chilled)
Equipment: Foil

neutral oil, for cooking
1 head of garlic
6 large aubergines (eggplants)
8 tablespoons natural yoghurt
2 tablespoons lemon juice
flaky sea salt

Maple-pickled sultanas
4 tablespoons maple syrup
50 ml (1¾ fl oz/3½ tablespoons)
sherry vinegar
1 teaspoon flaky sea salt
100 ml (3½ fl oz/scant ½ cup)
water
50 g (1¾ oz) sultanas
(golden raisins)

Garam masala onions
3 large onions, halved and thinly
sliced towards the root end
1 tablespoon garam masala

Ideas for dipping
If I'm serving the Advanced Player
Garlic Bread on page 120
alongside this, I'd serve something
fresh like endive or chicory
(Belgian endive) leaves.
If not, pitta bread or toasted
flatbreads work well.

I love the way aubergines (eggplants) are like, 'cook me wrong
and hate me forever'. To be fair, the aubergine did suffer as an
unwilling participant in many a sad veggie kebab situ. You can
see where she's coming from. All that's needed is to lob them on
the grill, whole, then scrape out their insides. I do also love grilled
strips of aubergine (see page 159), but that creamy flesh, smoked
and mashed with mellow garlic and billowy yoghurt will always
be my number one.

● Put the maple syrup, vinegar, salt and water in a saucepan
and bring to the boil, then pour over the sultanas (golden raisins)
in a heatproof bowl and let stand for 1 hour.
● Heat a frying pan (skillet) over a medium-low heat and add
a generous splash of oil. Add the onions with a pinch of salt and
cook, stirring, for 40 minutes, or until caramelised. Five minutes
before the end of cooking time, add the garam masala and
a splash of water. Cook, stirring, until the water has evaporated.
● Prepare a barbecue for two-zone cooking as described on
page 12, with medium heat.
● Cut the very top off the head of garlic to expose the cloves
and drizzle with oil. Wrap in foil and place over indirect heat.
● Place the aubergines (eggplants) over direct heat, adding a
chunk of wood (such as oak) to the coals if you wish. Close the lid
and leave the vents about a quarter open. Cook for 30 minutes,
turning the aubergines occasionally, until collapsed and black.
● Remove the aubergines and garlic from the grill, transfer the
aubergines to a bowl and cover. Allow them to steam and
cool a bit, then scrape out the flesh in a bowl, avoiding the skin,
with a splash of the juices.
● Mash the flesh with the garlic, yoghurt and lemon juice and
season with salt. Stir through the onions and sultanas and serve.

To cook indoors: You could roast the aubergines over a flame or
under a grill, and roast the garlic, but you won't get the smokiness.

Dips

Yoghurt, Sriracha Brown-buttered Corn and 'Nduja Crumbs

Serves: 6
Cook and assembly time:
15 minutes

40 g (1½ oz) butter
2 × 196 g (7 oz) tins sweetcorn, drained
1 tablespoon sriracha
handful of chives, finely chopped
500 g (1 lb 2 oz/2 cups) cold thick Greek yoghurt

'Nduja crumbs
10 g (¼ oz) butter
25 g (¾ oz) 'nduja
100 g (3½ oz/scant 1 cup) panko breadcrumbs

Ideas for dipping
I like to serve this one with crisps e.g. tortilla chips, Pringles or crinkle cut crisps. Salt and vinegar and/or prawn cocktail are my favourites.

This has everything I love about a good dip: cold meets warm, spicy meets cooling, crunchy meets smooth. To keep the 'nduja crumbs crisp I serve them in a separate bowl, so that people can plunge first into the brown-buttered yoghurt situation, then move onto a crumb finish, to really layer up those flavours.

● Melt the butter for the crumbs in a frying pan (skillet) over a medium heat and add the 'nduja. Allow it to melt, breaking it up with a spoon, then add the breadcrumbs and fry until they've soaked up all the 'nduja flavour and are crisp.
● Melt the butter for the dip in a small saucepan over a medium heat and allow it to become brown and nutty, swirling it until you can see brown specks in the bottom of the pan and it smells lovely and toasty. Stir in the corn, sriracha and chives.
● Place the cold yoghurt into a serving bowl and top with the corn butter. Serve the 'nduja crumbs in a separate bowl for dipping, and crisps on the side.

Platters

Super Herbal Chicken Wings

Makes: 36 pieces
Prep: Marinate the wings up
to 24 hours ahead.
Cook and assembly time:
30 minutes
Equipment: Small blender, tongs

18 whole chicken wings,
separated into flats and drums
100 g (3½ oz/scant ½ cup)
Greek yoghurt
50 g (1¾ oz) butter

Marinade
6 garlic cloves
2 teaspoons ground coriander
large bunch of coriander (cilantro),
leaves and stalks
large bunch of basil, leaves
and stalks
small bunch of mint, leaves only
2 shallots, peeled
2 lemongrass stalks, outer layers
removed and stalks sliced
thumb of ginger, peeled
2 fresh green chillies
50 ml (1¾ fl oz/3½ tablespoons)
lime juice
grated zest of 2 limes
50 ml (1¾ fl oz/3½ tablespoons)
neutral oil
generous pinch of flaky sea salt

To serve
lime wedges
coriander (cilantro) leaves

This is probably my favourite wings recipe, and I've written a fair few because chicken wings are perfect party food: inexpensive, easy to cook and transformed by their time over fire.

Here they are marinated and dressed with a vigorous, fragrant sauce singing with herbs, lemongrass and lime. I find the combination of the aromatics, creamy yoghurt and rich butter irresistible, especially on crackly chicken skin, still fizzing from the grill.

● Combine all the marinade ingredients in a small blender and whizz to a paste.
● Combine the wings with two-thirds of the marinade and all the yoghurt and marinate in the fridge for as long as possible (up to 24 hours, if you have time).
● Prepare a barbecue for two-zone cooking as described on page 12, with the coals arranged in the centre of the barbecue and space around the edge.
● Once the barbecue is ready, arrange the wings in a circle around the coals, but not directly over them. Cook the wings, turning them every so often, until cooked through and caramelised. This will take about 30 minutes, and you can move the wings further into the centre as the coals burn down.
● Combine the butter and reserved marinade in a saucepan and melt together, warming through for a couple of minutes. Place the wings on a platter or dish then pour the butter over the cooked wings.
● Serve with lime wedges and coriander (cilantro).

To cook indoors: Cook under a preheated hot grill for about 20 minutes, turning the wings once, until cooked through and charred in places.

Platters

Sticky Scotch Bonnet and Citrus-smothered Lamb
with Confit Garlic and Peppers

Serves: 6
Prep: The lamb can be marinated up to 24 hours ahead.
Cook and assembly time: 3 hours
Equipment: Pestle and mortar, roasting tray, heatproof gloves, foil, pastry brush

---

1 medium lamb shoulder (bone-in), about 2 kg (4½ lb), any excess fat removed
4 red, orange or yellow (bell) peppers, trimmed, deseeded and cut into thick wedges
2 heads of garlic
juice of 2 oranges
juice of 2 lemons

Rub
1 tablespoon coriander seeds
½ tablespoon cumin seeds
½ tablespoon fennel seeds
grated zest of 2 oranges
grated zest of 2 lemons
grated zest of 2 limes
5 garlic cloves, grated to a paste
thumb of ginger, peeled and grated to a paste
2 sprigs of thyme, leaves picked
flaky sea salt

Glaze
100 ml (3½ fl oz/scant ½ cup) sweet chilli sauce or chilli jam
1 scotch bonnet chilli, deseeded (if you like) and finely chopped

When cooking a large piece of meat, it makes sense to me to harness the transformative properties of the fat released into the pan. As the lamb becomes pull-apart tender and its sticky glaze intensifies, veg confit in the rendered fat and citrus. What alchemy. The result is an impressive centrepiece with vegetables that spread like butter. Serve with flatbreads or roasted potatoes.

● Heat a frying pan (skillet) over a medium heat and add the whole spices. Toast, swirling the pan, until fragrant. Transfer to a mortar and crush to a powder with a pestle, then add the zests, garlic, ginger, thyme leaves and plenty of salt. Work to a paste.
● Score the lamb shoulder all over, at roughly 1 cm (½ inch) intervals, then smother it with the rub, working it into the meat. Leave to marinate for a couple of hours (or longer, if you wish).
● Prepare a barbecue for two-zone cooking as described on page 12, with medium heat.
● Place the lamb into a roasting tray and add the juices from all the citrus fruit into the bottom (not on the meat). Cover the tray with foil, then poke some holes in it to let some smoky flavour infuse. Place offset on the cooler side of the barbecue and close the lid, closing the top and bottom vents two-thirds of the way.
● Cook the lamb for about 1 hour, checking it at the 30-minute mark and topping up the charcoal if necessary.
● Add the (bell) peppers and garlic to the tray at the 2-hour mark, then re-cover and cook the lamb until tender, another hour.
● Combine the chilli sauce or jam with the scotch bonnet. Brush the lamb with the chilli sauce using a pastry brush and return to the barbecue, covered, for another 15 minutes, then uncover and cook for 10 minutes (with the lid down).
● Transfer to a platter and allow to rest for 15 minutes, covered with foil, then pull the lamb and drizzle the juices over the meat. Serve with the garlic and peppers.

To cook indoors: Cook at 180°C (350°F/gas 4) for 3 hours.

Platters

Spice-smothered Hasselback Squash (or Lamb Chops)
with Ricotta and Chilli Sauce

Serves: 4
Prep: The squash can be marinated up to 24 hours ahead, and the dressing can be made up to 8 hours ahead.
Cook and assembly time: 45 minutes
Equipment: Spice grinder or pestle and mortar, tongs

1 tablespoon cumin seeds
1 tablespoon coriander seeds
2 teaspoons fennel seeds
4 green cardamom pods, crushed and seeds removed
2 teaspoons dried chilli flakes
100 g (3½ oz/7 tablespoons) butter, softened
1 butternut squash (about 1 kg/ 2 lb 4 oz)
250 g (9 oz/1 cup) ricotta
flaky sea salt

Green dressing
1 fresh green chilli, finely chopped
4 tablespoons extra virgin olive oil
handful of coriander (cilantro), finely chopped
small handful of mint leaves, finely chopped
2 tablespoons lime juice
1 teaspoon caster (superfine) sugar

This is a version of a recipe I worked on for my last book, *Live Fire*, but which didn't make it into the final manuscript. I've since tweaked and refined it and it's become a bit of a staple.

To make this with lamb chops, combine half the spices with a splash of oil and some salt to make a paste, then toss with the lamb chops and marinate overnight. The next day, brush most of the marinade off the chops and cook them for a few minutes on each side over direct heat, moving them to one side if the fat is flaring up too much. Combine the remaining spices with 50 g (1¾ oz) melted butter and pour over the lamb chops to serve, along with the dressing and ricotta.

● Toast the cumin, coriander and fennel seeds in a dry frying pan (skillet) over a medium heat until fragrant. Grind or crush roughly with the cardamom seeds using a spice grinder or a pestle and mortar, then combine with the chilli flakes, butter and some salt.
● Hasselback the squash by cutting it in half lengthways and removing the seeds, then placing it cut side down on the surface with two wooden spoons either side (this will stop you cutting all the way through). Cut through the squash at intervals roughly 1 cm (½ inch) apart. Rub half of the spiced butter all over the squash.
● Prepare the barbecue for two-zone cooking as described on page 12. Add a piece of wood (such as oak), then cook the squash offset, skin side up, for 30 minutes, with the lid down and vents half closed. Turn the squash over halfway through to soften the skin, using tongs.
● Combine all the green dressing ingredients and season with salt and pepper (you can do this in a small blender). Set aside.
● Once the squash is cooked, top it with the remaining butter while still hot. Cut into thick wedges and arrange on a serving platter. Dot with the ricotta and top with the chilli dressing.

To cook indoors: Preheat the oven 180°C (350°F/gas 4) and roast the squash halves for 30–40 minutes, or until tender.

Sides

Soy Buttered Potatoes

Serves: 4–6
Cook and assembly time:
15 minutes

500 g (1 lb 2 oz) new potatoes
50 g (1¾ oz) butter
2 garlic cloves, smashed with
something heavy or the side
of a knife
2 tablespoons light soy sauce
handful of chives, chopped,
to garnish

This is a ridiculously simple side based on one of my favourite pasta dishes, which combines spaghetti with soy butter and starchy pasta water to create something so luscious it's hard to believe how little effort was involved. The richness of the butter brings out the sweetness of the soy sauce and an almost mushroomy quality. Give it a try and you'll see what I mean!

● Cook the potatoes in boiling salted water until almost tender but not quite cooked.
● Meanwhile, melt the butter in a saucepan and add the garlic, cooking for a couple of minutes. Stir in the soy sauce and 2 tablespoons of the potato cooking water, mixing until it emulsifies. Remove and discard the garlic.
● Prepare a barbecue for two-zone cooking as described on page 12. Place the potatoes over direct heat and cook, turning regularly, until crusty and cooked through. Baste them regularly with the soy butter mixture, moving away from the heat if the butter begins to burn/flare up.
● Combine the warm potatoes with any remaining soy garlic butter and sprinkle over the chives.

Sides

Herbal Cabbage Salad
with Avocado Cream

Serves: 4
Prep: The avocado cream can be made a few hours in advance and refrigerated.
Assembly time: 10 minutes
Equipment: Mandoline (not essential, but useful), small blender

1 medium to large white cabbage, quartered and cored
2 handfuls of tarragon, leaves picked
large handful of chives, very finely chopped
flaky sea salt

Avocado cream
4 ripe avocados, stoned and peeled
juice of 2 limes
2 garlic cloves, grated to a paste
6 tablespoons sour cream
pinch of sugar

Dressing
2½ tablespoons maple syrup
juice of 2 limes

The cabbage has been, for me, the most surprising vegetable. I adore it roasted, when its stalks succumb and soften and the frilly edges char, but I also love it like this – as a fresh, crunchy counterpart to something creamy and a little sweet.

This bright, refreshing salad is incredibly moreish. It feels healthy, yet luxurious, and it works with grilled meat, fish, halloumi, in tacos, in wraps and stuffed into pitta with any kind of kebab. I'm sure there are many more appropriate situations I've yet to discover. All hail the humble cabbage!

● Slice the cabbage very thinly. This is easiest using a mandoline, but can also be achieved with a vegetable peeler or a knife.
● Place the cabbage in a bowl with a pinch of salt and give it a scrunch with your hands to soften it.
● Combine the ingredients for the avocado cream in a small blender and whizz until smooth. Season to taste with salt.
● Combine the maple syrup and lime juice and whisk until smooth, then add to the cabbage with the tarragon and chives.
● Spread the avocado cream over a plate, then top with a nest of the cabbage.

Sides

Dreamy, Creamy White Beans
with Confit Garlic

Serves: 4
Prep: The confit garlic can be made up to a week in advance and refrigerated.
Cook and assembly time: 1 hour 30 minutes, plus overnight soaking
Equipment: Foil, small blender

250 g (9 oz) dried cannellini beans
1 sprig of thyme
1 sprig of rosemary
1 bay leaf
1 tablespoon double (heavy) cream
flaky sea salt and freshly ground black pepper

Confit garlic
2 large heads of garlic
extra virgin olive oil

It took me a while to come around to beans, and I think it was because I was always using them as a filler, rather than celebrating their unique qualities. Now, I love soaking them overnight to cook fresh. However, while I've been on a journey of beany discovery, some cooked bean brands have emerged that are actually worth the money (I like Bold Bean Co.) so if you don't have time to soak, they are a fantastic alternative.

Topped with silky confit garlic this is an elegant side dish, barbecue or no barbecue. I like to serve it with some bread, too – a smooshing vessel for both beans and cloves.

- Soak the dried beans overnight in cold water.
- Preheat the oven to 130°C (260°F/gas 2).
- Slice the tops off the heads of garlic to reveal the tops of the cloves and place into a small, shallow ovenproof dish, cut-sides down. Pour over oil until the bulbs are just covered. Cover tightly with foil and bake for 45 minutes to 1 hour, or until really soft.
- Remove from the oven and allow the garlic to cool in the oil, then transfer everything to a sealed container and chill.
- Adjust the oven temperature to 150°C (300°F/gas 2½).
- To cook the beans, drain them, transfer to a lidded ovenproof dish and cover again so that the water level is about 2.5 cm (1 inch) above the surface of the beans. Bring them gently to the boil, skimming off any scum, then add the thyme, rosemary, a generous pinch of salt and the bay. Bring to almost boiling point, then put the lid on and transfer to the oven for 1 hour to 1 hour 30 minutes, or until the beans are tender with a little liquid remaining.
- Strain, reserving both the juice and beans. Blend the beans with 100 ml (3½ fl oz/scant ½ cup) of the cooking liquid and the cream, then season with black pepper. Check the seasoning and add more salt, if needed.
- To serve, spread the beans over a large platter, then top with the heads of garlic cut in half across the cloves. Serve swirled with a generous amount of the garlic oil and lots of black pepper.

Desserts

Grilled Plums, Five-spice Crumble and Honey-rum Cream

Serves: 4
Prep: The crumble mix can be made a day in advance and stored in an airtight container.
Cook and assembly time: 25 minutes
Equipment: Electric whisk, baking tray, tongs

50 g (1¾ oz) cold unsalted butter, cubed
50 g (1¾ oz/scant ¼ cup) demerara sugar
50 g (1¾ oz/scant ⅓ cup) plain (all-purpose) flour
50 g (1¾ oz/generous ½ cup) rolled oats
½ teaspoon flaky salt
1 tablespoon Chinese five-spice

Plums
4 large plums
neutral oil, for brushing
2 tablespoons soft brown sugar (or any sugar will do)

Cream
150 ml (5 fl oz/⅔ cup) whipping cream
1 tablespoon runny honey
pinch of flaky sea salt
1 tablespoon dark rum

To serve
vanilla ice cream

I love a grilled stone fruit. It's a handy technique for fruits that perhaps aren't at their peak; at least, they're not those you'd be precious about eating straight up to savour their perfect ripeness.

Grilling brings out both sweetness and juice; softening and caramelising the fruit. I serve these plums with a quick crumble topping that's warm with Chinese five-spice, and a softly whipped cream hiding a kicker of rum. I also find that adding one form of cream to a dessert immediately makes me want to add another, which is why I often serve both whipped cream and ice cream. You'll never look back, I promise.

● Prepare a barbecue for two-zone cooking as described on page 12, with medium heat.
● To make the crumble, heat the oven to 200°C (400°F/gas 6).
● Combine the butter and sugar in a bowl and beat until combined with an electric whisk. Using your fingers, rub in the flour, oats, salt and five-spice – you're looking for lots of uneven lumps. Spread it onto a baking tray and bake in the oven for 10–15 minutes, or until golden.
● Slice the plums in half and remove the stones, then brush each plum all over with oil. Place cut-side down over direct heat and cook the plums for 5 minutes or so with the lid down and vents half closed, or until charred and soft.
● Turn the plums over with tongs, then sprinkle them with the sugar. Close the lid again and cook for a couple of minutes more, or until the sugar is melted.
● Using an electric whisk, whip the cream in a bowl until it's beginning to thicken. Add the honey, salt and rum and continue whisking to soft peaks.
● Serve the plums with the crumble and cream, and ice cream.

To cook indoors: Cook the plums cut side up under a hot grill for 10 minutes, or until soft and charred. Sprinkle with the sugar then return to the grill for a couple of minutes more.

Chilled 'n' Boozy Chocolate 'Cake'
with Sherbety Cherries

Serves: 8–10
Prep: The 'cake' can be made up to 2 days ahead and refrigerated
Assembly time: 10 minutes, plus setting time.
Equipment: 20 cm (8 inch) round cake tin, baking paper

300 g (10½ oz) very good-quality dark chocolate, finely chopped
300 ml (10 fl oz/1¼ cup) double (heavy) cream
1 tablespoon Amaretto
pinch of salt
200 g (7 oz) toasted almonds, roughly chopped
1 jar Luxardo cherries, drained and chopped (reserve the juice)
1 tablespoon cherry juice from the jar

Topping
200 g (7 oz) fresh cherries, pitted and halved
2 tablespoons golden caster (superfine) sugar
1 tablespoon sherry vinegar
3 tablespoons kirsch
300 g (10½ oz) crème fraîche

As you will have likely noticed, I generally keep desserts simple. I'm not a pastry chef, and I generally want something to really hit that spot without requiring much effort. This, then, is basically a boozy set ganache. Why not? I serve it with cherries macerated in kirsch and, crucially, sherry vinegar. It's the combination of the vinegar and sugar that gives them their sherbety quality and I can't get enough.

Are there slight Bakewell vibes here? Sure, but it's more a pleasant reminiscence than a reimagining, and of course, there's the addition of that undiluted, nut-flecked ganache; find the best dark chocolate you can and you shall be rewarded.

● Line the cake tin with baking paper.
● Melt the chocolate and cream together in a bain marie – place a heatproof bowl over a pan of gently simmering water, making sure the water isn't touching the base of the bowl, then add the chocolate and cream and let the chocolate gently melt.
● Remove from the heat and stir through the Amaretto, salt, almonds, cherries and cherry juice. Pour the mixture into the lined tin, allow to cool, then cover and refrigerate overnight.
● Thirty minutes before you want to serve, combine the cherries with sugar, vinegar and kirsch and set aside to macerate.
● Remove the 'cake' from the fridge 10 minutes before you want to serve it.
● Decant the crème fraîche into a bowl and gently fold some of the cherry macerating juice through it – you want it to be streaked with colour, not fully combined.
● Top the cake with the cherries and crème fraîche. Cut into slices to serve.

Desserts

Burnt Meringue, Vanilla Ice Cream and Olive Oil

Serves: 4
Prep and assembly time:
30 minutes
Equipment: Electric whisk, tongs

4 egg whites
200 g (7 oz/1¾ cups) icing
(powdered) sugar
1 tablespoon cornflour (cornstarch)

To serve
vanilla ice cream
very good olive oil
flaky sea salt

This is a very fun dessert that's perfect if you want to show off. A satiny, voluminous Swiss meringue is served in elegant swoops, then briefly burned with a glowing ember, to quickly toast the surface.

I love to serve this with vanilla ice cream and very good olive oil, just to blow people's minds a little further. If you're a food nerd like me, you might be familiar with the concept of new season olive oil, which is available from October to November, and would be the best thing you could use to dress this dessert. New season olive oil is the freshest and has the most potent and mesmerising flavour. If not, use the best extra virgin oil you can find. This isn't the time to use a regular olive oil.

- Prepare a pan of barely simmering water for making the meringues (you will place a bowl on top).
- Place the egg whites into a large heatproof bowl and whisk them briefly with an electric whisk, just to combine them. Place the bowl on top of the pan of water, ensuring the water doesn't touch the bottom of the bowl. Add the icing (powdered) sugar and beat with the electric whisk until you have a nice thick meringue that doesn't shift about when you move the bowl. Whisk in the cornflour (cornstarch) and set aside.
- Light a few coals in the barbecue and let them burn down to glowing hot embers. They need to be totally glowing all over – you want the coals to burn the meringue quickly and cleanly.
- Fill four bowls with scoops of vanilla ice cream, drizzle with olive oil and sprinkle with a few salt crystals.
- Scoop portions of the meringue onto each, then – very carefully – pick up a coal with your tongs and press it quickly into the side of each meringue portion, where it will leave a burn mark.
- Serve immediately!

nter

Crisp air, bright sunshine, and I'm a woollen bundle. The hastily lit grills keeps face and fingers toasty. Coal-roasted beetroots leak purple beetlejuice. A gentle infusion of smoke. Sausages braise as liquid blips. Sticky bits form. Smacked lips. A whole roasted cabbage bastes gently in butter – leaves caramelised as core softens. I serve ice cold MSG martinis indoors, bringing a succession of hot treats on their powerful tails. Leaves blow through the door behind me as I'm greeted by grins.

Winter

Today

Drinks
Ice cold MSG Martinis

Nibbles
Rules Bar Nuts

Dip
An OTT Whipped Cod's Roe Platter

Platter
Hedgehog Halloumi with Harissa and Pistachio

Side
A Turkish Riff on Smacked Cucumbers

Dessert
BBQ Banana Split with Miso-Sesame Crunch

Tomorrow

Next week

Drinks
Peach and Maple Old Fashioned

Nibbles
Aubergine Rolls with Walnuts, Caramelised
Onions and Herbs

Dip
An Elite Creamy Garlic and Caramelised
Onion Dip

Platter
Sticky Agrodolce Sausages

Side
Coal-baked Beetroot and Halloumi with
Sumac and Grape Dressing

Dessert
Sticky Toffee Pudding with Smoky Dates
and Bourbon

Drinks
Demerara and Star Anise Mojito

Nibbles
Lemony Grilled Olives

Dip
Squidgy Honey-slicked Feta, Charred Bread
and Green Tahini

Platter
Arayes Platter

Side
Whole BBQ Roasted Cabbages with Honey,
Marmite and Butter

Dessert
The Ambassador's Mille-feuille

Drinks

Demerara and Star Anise Mojito

Makes: 2
Assembly time: 5 minutes
Equipment: Cocktail shaker, muddler (or a rolling pin), strainer, sieve
Glass: Short, like an Old Fashioned

---

50 ml (1¾ fl oz/3½ tablespoons) lime juice
30 g (1 oz/generous 2 tablespoons) demerara sugar
handful of mint leaves
ice cubes
120 ml (4 fl oz/½ cup) dark rum
2 star anise

I'm not sure how fashionable mojitos are these days, but I couldn't care less. That combination of muddled sugar, lime, mint and rum makes something so zingy-fresh yet warm at the same time; it's a banger whatever the weather. I love to do a variation for colder months using demerara sugar for a slightly more toasty caramel flavour, and star anise, which adds an intriguing backnote.

● Muddle the lime juice, sugar and mint leaves in a cocktail shaker, making sure you give everything a really good crush.
● Add a handful of ice cubes and the rum and shake until condensation appears on the outside of the shaker.
● Set up a sieve over a jug or other container and strain the drink through it, using a cocktail strainer. This is called double straining, and just eliminates any chance of getting bits of star anise floating in your drink.
● Serve the cocktails over ice.

Drinks

Ice-cold MSG Martinis

Makes: 2
Assembly time: 5 minutes,
plus chilling time
Equipment: Cocktail shaker,
strainer, cocktail sticks
Glass: Martini glass

---

120 ml (4 fl oz/½ cup) gin
25 ml (¾ fl oz/generous
1½ teaspoons) olive brine
pinch of MSG
60 ml (2 fl oz/4 tablespoons)
French vermouth
ice cubes
2 green olives, such as Nocellara,
to serve

I usually drink my martinis with a twist, but have recently dabbled with the dirty, and for those who also enjoy the murky brine, this is the ultimate version. A word of warning: this is not the kind of drink to serve more than one of, particularly when there's a barbecue involved.

● Put the glasses in the freezer an hour before you want to make the martinis, ideally. Any time is better than no time, however.
● Combine the gin, brine, MSG and vermouth in a cocktail shaker with a handful of ice cubes. Stir until condensation appears on the outside of the shaker, then strain into the ice-cold glasses.
● Serve with olives in the glasses or skewered on cocktail sticks.

Drinks

Peach and Maple Old Fashioned

Makes: 4
Assembly time: 5 minutes, plus infusing time
Equipment: Cocktail shaker
Glass: Short, like an Old Fashioned

1½ tablespoons maple syrup
250 ml (8 fl oz/1 cup) bourbon
dash of angostura bitters
1 peach and orange or plain peach teabag
ice cubes
soda water (optional)
strips of orange peel, to garnish

While I do enjoy a herbal or fruit tea of an evening, I'm also impressed by how well teabags infuse their flavour into booze. Since peaches can be an unreliable fruit, I find that using teabags instead gets the job done very consistently.

● Combine the maple syrup, bourbon and angostura bitters in a cocktail shaker and shake to combine.
● Pour into a bottle or other sealable container and add the peach teabag. Set aside to infuse for a couple of hours or up to overnight.
● Discard the teabag, then pour over ice into 4 glasses, adding a dash of soda water, if using, and a strip of orange peel.

Nibbles

Aubergine Rolls
with Walnuts, Caramelised Onions and Herbs

Makes: 12
Prep: The aubergines and filling can be made and assembled up to 8 hours in advance.
Cook and assembly time: 1 hour
Equipment: Tongs, small blender or pestle and mortar

neutral oil, for cooking and brushing
2 onions, thinly sliced
2 garlic cloves, grated to a paste
1 tablespoon lemon juice
3 medium aubergines (eggplants), cut lengthways into 0.5–1 cm (¼–½ inch)-thick strips – the longer variety of aubergines is easier to work with
100 g (3½ oz) walnuts
2 teaspoons ground coriander
½ teaspoon fenugreek seeds, crushed
2 teaspoons ground cumin
1 teaspoon hot paprika
2 teaspoons pomegranate molasses
small handful of coriander (cilantro) leaves, finely chopped
small handful of parsley leaves, finely chopped
small handful of mint leaves, finely chopped
small handful of basil leaves, finely chopped
sea salt and ground white pepper

These aubergine (eggplant) rolls are based on nigvziani badrijani, a Georgian appetiser made with walnuts and a spice mixture called khmeli-suneli. I've found it impossible to do justice to certain Georgian dishes due to the unavailability of regional spices and herbs, so this is a version I've tinkered with over the years that's moved away from the traditional.

The soft, pliable aubergine lengths are rolled around a rich mixture of walnuts, herbs and caramelised onions. It takes a little effort, but they can be made in advance and stored in the fridge.

● Heat a dash of oil in a frying pan (skillet) over a low heat, add the onions with a pinch of salt and cook for 40 minutes, stirring, until caramelised. Remove from the heat and chop finely.
● Prepare a barbecue for two-zone cooking as described on page 12, with medium-low heat.
● Combine the grated garlic and lemon in a bowl and set aside.
● Brush the aubergine (eggplant) strips with a little oil and season with salt. Cook the aubergine strips gently offset on the cooler side of the barbecue (but not too far away from the coals) for about 10 minutes on each side until they are soft and charred. Once cooked, roll them up and set aside.
● Gently toast the walnut pieces in a dry frying pan (skillet) over a medium-low heat, taking care not to burn them.
● Transfer the nuts to a small blender or mortar and blitz or crush the walnuts to a crumbly consistency, before mixing in the chopped onions, garlic and lemon, spices, pomegranate molasses and herbs and seasoning with salt and white pepper.
● Unroll the aubergine strips and place a teaspoon full of nut mixture on one end, then re-roll.
● To serve, arrange the aubergine rolls on a serving platter for everyone to help themselves.

To cook the aubergines indoors: Preheat a griddle pan over a high heat for 5 minutes, then cook the aubergine slices in batches.

Nibbles

Rules Bar Nuts

Serves: 4
Prep: The nuts can be made several days ahead and stored in an airtight container.
Cook and assembly time: 10 minutes, plus cooling time

250 g (9 oz) mixed nuts
1 tablespoon neutral oil
10 g (⅓ oz) curry powder
75 g (2½ oz/5 tablespoons) salted butter
75 g (2½ oz) runny honey
25 g (1 oz/2 tablespoons) caster (superfine) sugar
3 g cayenne pepper
3 g smoked paprika
1 tablespoon flaky sea salt

I've had many astonishingly good cocktails in London's Rules Bar over the years, and during that time I've become friends with Brian Silva, the incredibly talented man who shaped the bar over many years and has recently returned as its guardian.

After many unsuccessful attempts to recreate their bar nuts recipe, I decided to ask Brian if his kitchen would be prepared to share the recipe, and here we are! A huge thank you to Brian and Rules Bar for this recipe, which has been honed and tweaked over many years. These are incredibly addictive.

● Preheat the oven to 180°C (350°F/gas 4) and spread the nuts out on a baking tray.
● Toss the nuts with the oil and the curry powder and roast in the oven for 10 minutes, turning them halfway through.
● Transfer to a saucepan with the butter, honey, sugar and remaining spices and the salt. Stir and cook over a medium-low heat for about 10 minutes. Once coated and bubbling, transfer to a baking tray, spread them out and allow to cool fully.

Nibbles

Lemony Grilled Olives

Serves: 4
Cook and assembly time:
10 minutes
Equipment: Roasting dish, grilling basket or foil

½ lemon
250 g (9 oz) pitted mixed olives
needles from a sprig of rosemary
2 garlic cloves
1 tablespoon neutral oil such as vegetable or groundnut
½ tablespoon pul biber or any other mild chilli flakes

Olives are a fairly standard nibble, but have you ever tried grilling them? They wrinkle and intensify, and you can add all sorts of flavourings. I like to cook them in a little foil parcel on the barbecue, where they become lightly smoky and adorably shrivelled.

● Prepare a barbecue for two-zone cooking as described on page 12.
● Slice the lemon into rounds, reserving the end piece for serving. Pop out any pips.
● Combine the olives, rosemary needles, whole garlic cloves, oil and pul biber and mix well.
● Place the olives into a roasting dish, a grilling basket or a parcel made from foil and cook for 8–10 minutes, or until the olives are wrinkled.
● Remove the garlic cloves, lemon slices and any charred bits of herb, and transfer the olives to a serving bowl. Squeeze over the juice of the remaining piece of lemon and serve.

To cook indoors: Preheat the oven to 220°C (430°F/gas 9). Combine the olives in an ovenproof dish with the flavourings and roast in the oven for 10–15 minutes.

Dips

An OTT Whipped Cod's Roe Platter

Serves: 4-6
Prep: The whipped roe can be made up to 24 hours in advance
Cook and assembly time: 25 minutes
Equipment: Small blender, sieve

1 large piece of smoked cod's roe (about 350 g/12 oz)
50 g (1¾ oz) crustless white bread
splash of milk
½ small red onion
3 tablespoons lemon juice, plus grated zest of 1 lemon
50 g (1¾ oz) crème fraîche
150 g (5½ oz/scant ⅔ cup) mascarpone
100 ml (3½ fl oz/scant ½ cup) extra virgin olive oil
flaky sea salt and white pepper

Herby crème fraîche
150g (5½ oz/scant ⅔ cup) crème fraîche
small handful of chives, finely chopped
small handful of tarragon leaves, chopped
small handful of dill fronds, chopped
grated zest of 1 lemon and a small squeeze of juice

To garnish
salmon roe or caviar
shichimi togarashi
pickled chillies
pickled silverskin onions

I love all whipped cod's roe, from the pale-peach coloured 'white tarama' to the more lurid Pink Panther-hued corner-shop tubs. My recipe is a little different to many out there, because I use mascarpone. Someone once told me they used it to thicken their fishy dip and while I was bemused at the time, I now can't do without it. This is thick, smoky and unapologetic, and I like to really go mad with it, throwing all the garnishes, herbs and crisp varieties into the mix. Here, I've served it with sliced fennel rubbed with lemon juice as well as salt and vinegar crisps (smoky bacon crisps also work very well) and toasted pitta bread. We've all done tasteful cod's roe, guys – it's time to get wild.

● Peel the skin from the roe – this is easier if you are patient with it, and quite satisfying overall.
● Tear the bread into pieces and combine with the splash of milk to soften.
● Finely grate the onion, then strain in a sieve and reserve the juice.
● Combine the roe, bread and milk, lemon juice, onion juice, crème fraîche and mascarpone in a small blender and whizz to a paste. Add the oil with the motor running, then season with white pepper. Transfer to the fridge for 1 hour to firm up a bit.
● Make the herby crème fraîche by combining all the ingredients with some salt and pepper.
● To serve, swoop some of the crème fraîche onto a plate, then swoosh the whipped roe next to it. Top the roe with caviar and a light sprinkle of togarashi, then serve the pickled chillies, onions crisps, fennel and bread around the outside.

Dips

Squidgy Honey-slicked Feta, Charred Bread and Green Tahini

Serves: 4
Prep: The feta parcels can be assembled up to 24 hours ahead (stored in the fridge); the green tahini can be made up to 8 hours ahead (also chilled).
Cook and assembly time: 30 minutes
Equipment: Foil, tongs, small blender

400 g (14 oz) feta (2 blocks)
grated zest of 2 lemons
2 tablespoons pul biber
1 teaspoon dried mint
2 tablespoons honey
olive oil, for drizzling
in each parcel
1 teaspoon nigella seeds

Green tahini
1 garlic clove, grated to a paste
handful of coriander (cilantro) leaves and stalks, chopped
handful of parsley leaves, chopped
150 g (5½ oz) tahini
½ teaspoon ground cumin
squeeze of lemon juice
60 ml (2 fl oz/¼ cup) cold water
flaky sea salt and freshly ground black pepper

Ideas for dipping
chunky bread, e.g., focaccia (see page 124 for my Skillet Focaccia) or sourdough, torn into chunks

Feta takes on a new personality when it's warmed through, becoming jiggly-soft and scoop-able. I love to squish it onto good, charred bread with a chaser of herbaceous green tahini. A rich, luscious combination.

● Prepare a barbecue for two-zone cooking as described on page 12.
● Lay out two overlapping sheets of foil like a cross then place one piece of feta inside. Top with half of the other ingredients then wrap to secure. Repeat with the second block of feta and another two overlapping sheets of foil, to make two foil parcels.
● Place the foil parcels offset on the barbecue and cook for 15 minutes with the lid on and vents half closed.
● To make the green tahini, put the garlic, coriander (cilantro), parsley, tahini, cumin and lemon juice in a small blender with some salt and pulse to a paste. Slowly drizzle in the cold water with the motor running or until you have a consistency of sour cream. Season with salt and pepper.
● Char your bread on the barbecue, then remove it, along with the feta. Serve the feta parcels with the green tahini and charred bread.

To cook indoors: Preheat the oven to 180°C (350°F/gas 4) and cook the feta parcels on a baking tray for 15 minutes. Char the bread on a griddle pan.

Dips

An Elite Creamy Garlic and Caramelised Onion Dip

Serves: 8–10
Prep: Onions can be caramelised up to 24 hours in advance.
Confit garlic can be prepared up to two weeks in advance and refrigerated.
Cook and assembly time:
45 minutes, plus extra for the confit garlic (see method on page 140)

---

1 × 150 g (5½ oz) pack Boursin garlic and herb cheese
165 g (5¾ oz/generous ¾ cup) cream cheese
120 g (4¼ oz) sour cream
small squeeze of lemon juice
handful of chives, very finely chopped
crisps and/or focaccia, to serve

Caramelised onions

50 g (1¾ oz) butter
4 onions, peeled and thinly sliced with the tip of the knife pointing towards the root
pinch of caster (superfine) sugar
100 ml (3½ fl oz/scant ½ cup) brine from sweet pickled gherkins
a few cloves of confit garlic (see page 140)
flaky sea salt

This is based on one corner of that famous supermarket 4-way we all know and secretly love. I've ramped up the flavour and added some luxe touches in the form of confit garlic and cream cheese, plus an alluring acidity from pickled gherkin brine. It will ruin all other cream cheese and garlic dips forever, I'm afraid. Serve with sturdy crisps or charred wedges of the Skillet Focaccia on page 124.

● First, prepare the onions by melting the butter in a frying pan (not cast-iron) over a medium-low heat. Add the onions, sugar and a pinch of salt and allow to cook slowly and caramelise, stirring often, for 30 minutes.
● At this point the onions will be well on their way to caramelising. Add the brine to deglaze the pan, scraping up any oniony bits from the bottom, and allow the liquid to bubble down and be absorbed into the onions. Once all the liquid has gone, remove the onions from the pan and set aside to cool. Once cooled, finely chop with the confit garlic.
● In a large bowl, combine the Boursin, cream cheese, sour cream and lemon juice. Using a wooden spoon or spatula, mix everything together really well, beating it until it's a little lighter and fluffier. Stir through most of the chives, reserving a few for garnish, stir in the caramelised onions and check the seasoning – it will likely want a pinch of salt.
● Decant into a serving bowl and top with the remaining chives. Serve with wedges of warmed or charred focaccia and/or crisps.

Platters

Sticky Agrodolce Sausages

Serves: 4
Cook and assembly time:
45 minutes
Equipment: Tongs, roasting tin,
heatproof gloves, pastry brush

---

2 onions, peeled and quartered
(leave the root intact)
2 red or yellow (bell) peppers,
deseeded and quartered
8 pork sausages
1 × 400 g (14 oz) tin chopped
tomatoes
400 g (14 oz) cooked
chickpeas (garbanzo beans)
(drained weight)
1 teaspoon fennel seeds
3 tablespoons red wine vinegar
3 tablespoons honey
a good slug of olive oil
flaky sea salt and freshly ground
black pepper

This dish is pure sweet 'n' salty magic. Charring the veg and sausages first develops some scrappy edges, which are essential to the character of the dish. An everyday traybake she ain't. Everything becomes rich and sticky as the olive oil and honey work together to give the tomatoes a jamminess, as if they've been cooked long and slow. This is also very good the next day, eaten straight from the fridge (or reheated and served with a fried egg, should a sore head require it).

● Prepare a barbecue for two-zone cooking as described on page 12, with medium-high heat.
● Place the onions, peppers and sausages over direct heat and cook for about 5 minutes until the sausages are browned and the vegetables charred, turning them with tongs.
● Transfer to a roasting tin with the tinned tomatoes, chickpeas (garbanzo beans) and fennel seeds and give everything a mix.
● Combine the vinegar and honey, then brush the mixture over the sausages, drizzling any remaining mixture into the vegetables and chickpeas. Season well and add a generous slug of olive oil over everything.
● Place back on the barbecue over indirect heat and allow to cook, uncovered but with the lid closed and the bottom vents two-thirds closed for 30 minutes.
● To serve, arrange the sausages on a serving platter with the pepper and chickpea mixture around them.

To cook indoors: Char the onions and peppers under a hot grill or in a preheated griddle pan until blackened in places. Preheat the oven to 200°C (400°F/gas 6) and cook the sausages and vegetables in the oven for 30 minutes.

Platters

Hedgehog Halloumi
with Harissa and Pistachio

Serves: 6
Prep: The pistachio sauce can be made up to 8 hours in advance.
Cook and assembly time:
30 minutes
Equipment: Small blender, pastry brush, tongs

70 g (2½ oz) shelled unsalted pistachios
2 teaspoons lemon juice
1 garlic clove
6 tablespoons extra virgin olive oil
large handful of basil leaves
pinch of mild dried chilli flakes
sea salt

Salad
1 tablespoon lemon juice
2 tablespoons extra virgin olive oil
pinch of salt
pinch of caster (superfine) sugar
1 teaspoon sumac
handful of parsley leaves
handful of coriander
(cilantro) leaves
handful of basil leaves
handful of mint leaves
1 red onion, very thinly sliced

Halloumi
2 × 250 g (9 oz) blocks of halloumi
olive oil, for brushing
apricot or peach jam, for glazing

To serve
6 flatbreads or pitta
2 tablespoons harissa
250 g (9 oz/1 cup) natural yoghurt
extra apricot or peach jam

I learned about this method of cooking halloumi from Georgina Hayden's book, Taverna: Recipes from a Cypriot Kitchen, and I haven't looked back. Cross-hatching it allows the middle to soften but the corners (of which there are now many) become temptingly charred. I serve it glazed with jam, with a pistachio and basil sauce and a herb salad. This is halloumi given the glow-up she deserves.

● Prepare a barbecue for two-zone cooking as described on page 12.
● Combine all the ingredients for the pistachio and basil sauce in a small blender and whizz to a sauce. Season with salt.
● To make the dressing for the salad, combine the lemon juice, olive oil, salt, sugar and sumac in a clean lidded jar or bowl and shake or whisk to combine.
● Combine the herbs and onion for the salad in a bowl and mix with the dressing.
● Score the halloumi in a criss-cross pattern, about 2 cm (¾ inch) deep with the marks about 1 cm (½ inch) apart. Brush lightly with olive oil and place over direct heat, cooking for 3–5 minutes each side and turning with tongs, or until lightly charred. Glaze with apricot jam.
● Serve the halloumi with warmed flatbreads or pitta, the dressed salad, harissa, yoghurt and extra jam.

To cook indoors: Pop the halloumi under a hot grill and grill for a few minutes on each side.

Platters

Arayes Platter

Makes: 12 small arayes, easily halved
Prep: The filling and sauces can be prepped up to 8 hours or so in advance and refrigerated.
Cook and assembly time: 45 minutes
Equipment: Small blender, pastry brush, tongs

6 pitta breads, cut in half to make two pockets
neutral oil, for brushing

Filling
1 kg (2 lb 4 oz) minced (ground) lamb
bunch of parsley leaves, finely chopped
bunch of coriander (cilantro) leaves and stalks, finely chopped
4 garlic cloves, grated to a paste
1 small onion, very finely chopped
2 tablespoons Lebanese seven-spice
2 teaspoons hot paprika

Arayes (a Levantine street food) are ideal party food – self-contained kebabs where the meat is cooked inside the bread. They're simple to cook, convenient to hold and incredibly easy to eat.

Spiced minced (ground) lamb is stuffed into pitta bread and grilled, so that the bread becomes crisp while the inside stays really juicy. I love serving them with a trio of sauces: a zippy zhoug, creamy tahini yoghurt and fiery harissa mayonnaise.

Try to get the lovely soft, round pitta breads for this, if you can, rather than the harder slipper-shaped ones.

● Prepare a barbecue for two-zone cooking as described on page 12.
● Whisk together the yoghurt, tahini and lemon juice in a bowl. Add the other ingredients, whisking until smooth, then set aside.
● Combine all the ingredients for the zhoug in a small blender and whizz to combine. Season with some salt and set aside.
● Combine the mayo and harissa in a bowl with salt and set aside.
● Mix all the ingredients for the filling together, then stuff it inside the pitta halves, taking care not to over-stuff them as they then won't cook in the middle. Brush the outside of the pitta with oil. Cut each pitta half in half again so that you have lots of stuffed quarters of pitta (if you're using oval-shaped pittas, leave them as halves).
● Cook the stuffed pittas cut-side down for a few minutes over direct heat until they begin to sizzle and char – you'll need to stay with them and shift them just to the other side of the coals once the fat begins to melt and drip. Cook for 5 or so minutes on each side or until cooked through – you can test them by inserting a skewer into the thickest part and touching the skewer to your lip – if it's warm, it's cooked.
● Serve the arayes on a platter with the sauces and let everyone help themselves.

To cook indoors: Cook the stuffed pittas on a hot griddle pan.

Tahini-yoghurt sauce

200 g (7 oz/generous ¾ cup)
full-fat natural Greek yoghurt
4 tablespoons tahini
20 ml (½ fl oz) lemon juice
2 garlic cloves, crushed
1 teaspoon dried mint
½ teaspoon caster (superfine)
sugar
1 teaspoon flaky sea salt
50 ml (1¾ fl oz/3½ tablespoons)
very cold water

Zhoug

2 fresh green chillies
large bunch of coriander (cilantro)
smaller bunch of parsley
½ teaspoon crushed green
cardamom seeds (from pods)
1 teaspoon ground cumin
3 tablespoons extra virgin olive oil
1 tablespoon lemon juice or white
wine vinegar
3 garlic cloves
2 teaspoons pul biber

Harissa mayo

150 g (5½ oz/¾ cup) mayonnaise
1 heaped tablespoon harissa

Sides

A Turkish Riff on Smacked Cucumbers

Serves: 4
Prep: The dressing can be mixed several hours in advance.
Cook and assembly time:
10 minutes
Equipment: Cleaver, rolling pin, or something heavy, for smacking the cucumbers

---

2 of those small cucumbers you get in Middle Eastern grocers or 1 large English cucumber
3 garlic cloves, crushed
1 teaspoon dried Urfa chilli
1 tablespoon red wine vinegar
1 tablespoon extra virgin olive oil
1 teaspoon flaky sea salt
1 tablespoon za'atar

This recipe was inspired by the super-fresh chopped salads of Turkish kebab restaurants, and the smacked cucumbers of Szechuan Province, China. The method of smacking the cucumber leaves it with lots of jagged, raggedy edges, which then enthusiastically hoover up the dressing.

Instead of the traditional Chinese flavourings of garlic, vinegar and chilli oil, I've used the mild, sun-roasted Urfa chilli and good red wine vinegar along with za'atar. This dish bears little resemblance to either the Turkish or Chinese originals, but it is a bold little side that works well with anything kebab-ish.

● Halve the cucumbers then place them seed side down on a chopping board.
● Smack them with the side of a cleaver or something else (a rolling pin will do a good job) until they're cracked but not obliterated.
● Chop into 2 cm (¾ inch) lengths and mix with all the other ingredients.

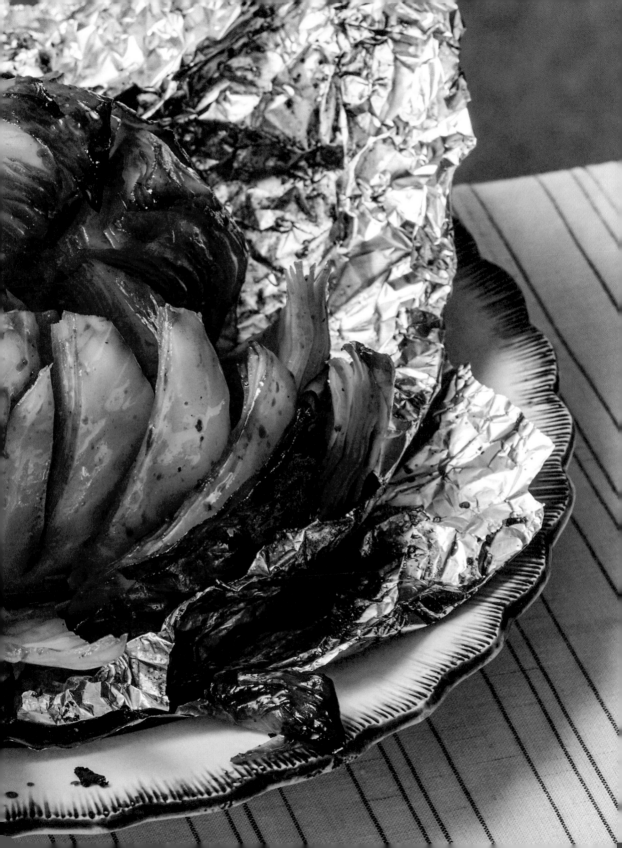

Sides

Whole BBQ Roasted Cabbages
with Honey, Marmite and Butter

Serves: 4–6
Prep: The cabbages can
be wrapped an hour or
so in advance.
Cook and assembly time:
1–2 hours
Equipment: Foil

2 small white cabbages
(these should be small enough to
hold comfortably in one hand,
about 700 g/1 lb 9 oz)
100 g (3½ oz/7 tablespoons)
salted butter
1 tablespoon Marmite
1 tablespoon honey
juice of ½ lemon
1 teaspoon ground white pepper
lemon wedges, to serve

As previously mentioned, I have a serious soft spot for cabbage, and I'm always looking for new ways to cook it. This is a total revelation. Whole cabbages are wrapped with a mixture of Marmite, sticky honey and – my one true forever love – BUTTER. They slowly roast on the barbecue, softening and collapsing into tender folds. It really is something special.

You can also replace the Marmite with a couple of tablespoons of 'nduja for a meaty version, or try a lemony mixed herb iteration.

● Prepare a barbecue for two-zone cooking as described on page 12, with medium-high heat.
● Bring a pan of water to the boil (large enough to hold the cabbage). Par-boil the whole cabbage for 5 minutes, then drain.
● Make four cuts into the top of each cabbage in a cross shape, about three-quarters of the way through, taking care not to cut all the way through.
● Melt the butter in a saucepan over a low heat, then add the Marmite and honey, mixing until everything's combined. Add the lemon juice and white pepper and mix well.
● Arrange two overlapping sheets of foil in a cross shape. Place a cabbage onto the centre of the sheets. Repeat with the second cabbage. Brush the mixture inside and all over the cabbages, and, once well coated, pour the remainder into the gaps. Wrap very well, then place over indirect heat for 1–2 hours, or until soft.
● Unwrap the cabbages on a baking tray or plate to catch all the precious juices, which can then be poured over to serve. Serve with lemon wedges for squeezing.

To cook indoors: Preheat the oven to 200°C (400°F/gas 6) and bake the foil-wrapped cabbages on a baking tray for 2 hours.

Coal-baked Beetroot and Halloumi
with Sumac and Grape Dressing

Serves: 4
Prep: The dressing can be made several hours in advance, but add the grapes just before serving.
Cook and assembly time:
1 hour 15 minutes
Equipment: Foil, tongs

500 g (1 lb 2 oz) medium beetroot (beets) (a similar size, ideally, to ensure they cook through in the same time)
neutral oil, for rubbing
225 g (8 oz) halloumi
flaky sea salt

Sumac and grape dressing
1 tablespoon pomegranate molasses
1 tablespoon lemon juice
4 tablespoons extra virgin olive oil
1 garlic clove, grated to a paste
1 teaspoon honey or caster (superfine) sugar
1 tablespoon sumac
10 seedless black grapes, halved

I never thought I'd see the day when I'd be excited about beetroot (beets) again, if I'm honest, but coal-baked beetroots are just SO much more interesting than beetroots cooked any other way. They become supremely tender, their plum colour preserved perfectly under feathery skins, which are easily rubbed away after cooking. They are concentrated, yet somehow less aggressively so than after roasting. It really is a transformation.

I serve them with a dressing of sparky sumac, treacly pomegranate molasses and grapes. I love to add some halloumi into the mix for contrast and because, well, I simply love halloumi.

● Prepare a barbecue for two-zone cooking as described on page 12, letting the flames die down to glowing embers.
● Rub the beetroots (beets) with a splash of oil and season them with salt, then wrap each one in foil. Place the beetroots right at the edge of the hot embers, so they're touching them but not right in the middle. Leave them alone, turning them around occasionally, until cooked. This will take about 1 hour, depending on the size of the beetroots. They're cooked when a skewer can be pushed easily into the beetroot.
● Combine all the ingredients for the dressing except for the grapes with some salt in a lidded jar or bowl and shake to combine. Add the grapes.
● Once the beetroots are cooked, add a few more coals if necessary, to cook the halloumi. Rub the halloumi with a little oil and cook over direct heat for a minute or so on each side, until charred and soft.
● Carefully unwrap the beetroots, rub the skins off and chop into wedges. Arrange on a platter and spoon over the dressing with the halloumi.

To cook indoors: To cook the beetroots in the oven, preheat the oven to 200°C (400°F/gas 6), wrap the beetroots in foil as above and roast for 45 minutes, or until tender.

Desserts

Sticky Toffee Pudding
with Smoky Dates and Bourbon

Serves: 8
Cook and assembly time: 1 hour
Equipment: 22 cm (8 ½ inch) square, 5 cm (2 inches) deep baking dish, plus another dish or rack, electric whisk

200 g (7 oz) pitted dates, roughly chopped
150 ml (5 fl oz/⅔ cup) just-brewed lapsang souchong tea
1 teaspoon vanilla bean paste or extract
90 g (3 oz/6 tablespoons) unsalted butter, softened, plus extra for greasing
2 tablespoons black treacle (molasses)
100 g (3½ oz/generous ½ cup) light muscovado sugar
2 eggs, at room temperature
175 g (6 oz/1 ⅓ cups) self-raising flour
1 teaspoon bicarbonate of soda (baking soda)
85 ml (3 fl oz/⅓ cup) whole (full-fat) milk

Toffee sauce
1 tablespoon black treacle (molasses)
200 g (7 oz/1 cup) dark muscovado sugar
3 tablespoons bourbon
150 g (5½ oz/10½ tablespoons) unsalted butter
200 ml (7 fl oz/scant 1 cup) double (heavy) cream, plus extra to serve

A sticky toffee pudding should be properly gooey and rich, end of. I do not mess about when it comes to the depth of flavour here, adding dates soaked in smoky lapsang souchong and vanilla, and a toffee sauce boosted with bourbon. She pulls no punches.

● Grease the baking dish with butter.
● Combine the dates with the hot tea and vanilla in a bowl and set aside for 30 minutes.
● Prepare a barbecue for two-zone cooking as described on page 12, with medium heat.
● Mix the butter and treacle (molasses) in a bowl with an electric whisk to combine, then add the sugar and mix again. Add the eggs one at a time, beating after each addition until well incorporated. Gently fold in a third of the flour and all the bicarbonate of soda using a metal spoon, followed by a third of the milk. Repeat until all the flour and the milk have been used up.
● Mash the dates before folding them into the mixture with their liquid. Spoon the mixture into the buttered dish.
● Place the empty dish or a rack upside down on the opposite side of the coals, then place the sticky toffee pudding dish on top of it and close the lid (with the vents half closed). You are aiming for a temperature of around 175⁰ C (350⁰F). Cook for 50 minutes, or until a skewer inserted into the sponge comes out clean.
● To make the sauce, combine the treacle, muscovado sugar, bourbon, butter and half the cream in a saucepan and heat gently until the sugar has dissolved, then turn up the heat and cook until bubbling. Cook, stirring, for a few minutes. Remove from the heat and stir through the remaining cream.
● Allow the pudding to cool for 5 minutes before poking all over with a skewer and pouring over a quarter of the sauce. Leave for another 15 minutes before serving with the sauce and cream.

To cook indoors: Preheat the oven to 180°C (350°F/gas 4) and bake the pudding for 20–25 minutes.

Desserts

BBQ Banana Split
with Miso-Sesame Crunch

Serves: 4
Prep: The crumble mix can be made at least 8 hours ahead and stored at room temperature in an airtight container.
Cook and assembly time: 20 minutes
Equipment: Electric whisk, pastry brush, tongs

4 bananas
2 tablespoons melted butter
vanilla ice cream
a few maraschino cherries, if you like

Miso-sesame crunchy crumble
100 g (3½ oz/7 tablespoons) cold unsalted butter, cubed
100 g (3½ oz/scant ½ cup) demerara sugar
2 teaspoons white miso paste
100 g (3½ oz/⅔ cup) plain (all-purpose) flour
50 g (1¾ oz/½ cup) rolled oats
4 tablespoons finely chopped hazelnuts
4 tablespoons black sesame seeds

A banana split is so kitsch and joyful it's hard to resist, particularly when the bananas are rendered golden from the grill and topped with a miso-turbo-ed nutty, crunchy crumble that's full of butter and sesame.

● Prepare a barbecue for two-zone cooking as described on page 12.
● Preheat the oven to 200°C (400°F/gas 6).
● Combine the butter, sugar and miso paste in a bowl and beat with an electric whisk until combined. Using your fingers, rub in the flour – you're looking for lots of uneven lumps. Stir in the oats, nuts and seeds.
● Spread the crumble mix onto a baking tray and bake in the oven for 10–15 minutes, or until golden, turning it halfway through with a spatula – it should be dark golden and will harden as it cools.
● Cut the bananas in half lengthways but don't peel them. Brush the cut sides with the melted butter. Place over direct heat, cut-side down, for 2–3 minutes, or until lightly charred.
● To serve, either arrange the grilled bananas on a platter and top with scoops of vanilla ice cream, cherries and the miso-sesame crunch, or arrange the elements in separate bowls. Either way, I let people help themselves.

To cook indoors: Brush the bananas with butter as above and cook in a preheated griddle pan cut-side down for a few minutes, or until lightly charred.

Desserts

The Ambassador's Mille-feuille

Serves: 6
Prep: Both the filling and cream will be fine stored in the fridge in their bags for at least a few hours.
Cook and assembly time:
45 minutes, plus cooling time.
Equipment: Baking paper, baking trays that fit inside each other, stand mixer or electric whisk, piping bags (optional but very useful for presentation here)

320 g (11½ oz) ready-rolled puff pastry sheet, preferably all-butter
50 g (1¾ oz) toasted hazelnuts, finely chopped
9 Ferrero Rocher
edible gold leaf
food-grade sparklers

Nutella filling
240 ml (8 fl oz/1 cup) cold double (heavy) cream
100 g (3½ oz/generous ¾ cup) icing (powdered) sugar, sifted
1 teaspoon vanilla bean paste
225 g (8 oz/1 cup) cream cheese
150 g (5½ oz) Nutella
pinch of flaky sea salt

Whipped cream for topping
300 ml (10 fl oz/1¼ cups) cold whipping cream
1 tablespoon cornflour (cornstarch)
1 tablespoon caster (superfine) sugar

This is obviously an OTT, silly dessert, but sometimes that's just the vibe I'm channelling. It also tastes amazing, so all bases covered. For those of us who grew up in the heyday of 90's ice cream cocktails, Viennettas and TV ads with pyramids of gold-wrapped chocs, this kind of childish magic is irresistible.

● Preheat the oven to 200°C (400°F/gas 6).
● Divide the pastry sheet into thirds so you have 3 roughly equal pieces measuring roughly 11.5 × 23 cm (4.5 × 9 inches).
● Place on a baking paper-lined baking tray, then top with more baking paper and a slightly smaller tray, to keep the pastry flat.
● Bake for 15–20 minutes until golden, then cool on a wire rack.
● Whip the cream in a stand mixer with a whisk attachment until soft peaks form, then scrape it out into a bowl, preserving the air.
● Whisk together the sifted icing (powdered) sugar, vanilla bean paste, cream cheese, Nutella and salt until the mixture turns a little paler and becomes creamy. Fold in the whipped cream with a rubber spatula until just combined.
● Transfer the Nutella filling to a piping (pastry) bag. Once full, twist the end of the bag, secure with a rubber band and chill.
● Whip the cream for the topping in a large bowl for 30 seconds, until beginning to thicken. Add the cornflour and sugar and continue whipping until it forms stiff peaks. Transfer to another piping bag as above and transfer to the fridge until needed.
● Place one pastry layer onto a serving plate. Snip the top off the Nutella piping bag to create a 2 cm/¼ inch opening, then pipe soft, wavy lines up and down the pastry.
● Top with the second layer of pastry and repeat with the remaining Nutella filling, then top with the final layer of pastry.
● Snip the top off the piping bag filled with whipped cream and pipe large balls of cream all over the top of the mille-feuille.
●Sprinkle over the chopped toasted hazelnuts, then top with the Ferrero Rocher and edible gold leaf. Just before serving, shove sparklers into the pastry and make your grand entrance!

Index

Acknowledgements

Putting out a 'second album' is notoriously nerve wracking, and I feel so lucky to have had the chance to do it. Of course, I depended on the talent, advice and support of so many others along the way. Thank you to my agent Kay Peddle, for her constant thoughtfulness, always considered advice and endless expertise. I'm so lucky to have you! To my editor Eve Marleau, what a joy it is to work with someone who genuinely loves what I'm doing and also makes me laugh so much along the way. Thank you. And thank you, too, Issy, for standing in at such a crucial time.

Merci beaucoup to the best in the business, Valerie Berry, for such incredible food styling. Your depth of knowledge is so inspiring and I am always in awe of your talent! Grilled potatoes 4eva. Thank you, too, Hanna Miller, I'm always overjoyed when I see your face in that kitchen! Thank you Rachel Vere, for your impeccable taste in props, your keen eye for detail and your excellent taste in books. I still haven't read The Bees – but I will!

To my babes Holly Catford and Robert Billington, thank you so much, as always! What a dream it is to work with you guys – you both just get better and better as humans and in your work. Thank you also to Rob's assistants Kate Anglestein and Jack Storer.

And finally, a huge thank you to everyone who has supported me during the time since my last book was published. Thank you to all of my readers, my family and my friends. It was a rocky road but I emerged a better person, and a *much* freer and more confident cook. This book is a celebration of eating with other people, and I hope it brings joy to you and yours.

About the Author

Helen Graves is a cook, food writer and editor. She specialises in barbecue, and is the author of the barbecue bible *Live Fire*, which was shortlisted for a Guild of Food Writers Award 2023. She is also editor of *Pit*, an independent food magazine. She won Editor of the Year: Food and Drink at the British Society of Magazine Editor's Awards 2020, and the Food Magazine Award at the Guild of Food Writers Awards 2023. Helen lives in South London with five barbecues and two cats.

Published in 2024 by
Hardie Grant Books,
an imprint of Hardie Grant
Publishing

Hardie Grant Books (London)
5th & 6th Floors
52–54 Southwark Street
London SE1 1UN

Hardie Grant Books (Melbourne)
Building 1, 658 Church Street
Richmond, Victoria 3121

hardiegrantbooks.com

British Library Cataloguing-in-
Publication Data. A catalogue
record for this book is available
from the British Library.

BBQ Days, BBQ Nights
ISBN: 978-1-78488-680-6

10 9 8 7 6 5 4 3 2 1

Publishing Director: Kajal Mistry
Commissioning Editor:
Eve Marleau
Design and art direction:
Holly Catford/Esterson Associates
Photographer: Robert Billington
Food Stylist: Valerie Berry
Prop Stylist: Rachel Vere
Copy editor: Laura Nickoll
Proofreader: Vicky Orchard
Indexer: Vanessa Bird
Production Controller:
Gary Hayes

Colour reproduction by p2d
Printed and bound in China by
Leo Paper Products Ltd.